Keto for Beginners

Start Your Ideal 7-day Keto Diet Plan to Lose Weight in 21 Days Now!

By Virginia Hoffman

Table of Contents

PREFACE:

Before you begin reading the first chapter, we would first like to give you a warm welcome and to thank you so much for choosing this book. "Keto for Beginners" is a book especially written for you and all those who want to improve their quality of life, starting with their relationship with food.

Often, people suffer from obesity, autoimmune disease, gastrointestinal disorders, and other health issues simply because they do not pay as much attention to what is on their plate as they should. However, since you have chosen this book it is safe to assume that you are the type of person who cares about his or her body. Rest assured, learning about the Ketogenic Diet can point you in the right direction.

Now, if you are reading this because you want to know what the Ketogenic Diet is, or that you have already heard about it and would like to know how to begin. This book will explain to you the steps on both.

The first chapter is all about what the Ketogenic diet is and what its basic rules are. It is explained in simpler terms and it provides you with the right foundational knowledge to help you do further research on your own.

The second chapter will share with you not one, but four 7-day meal plans to help you get started on the diet within the first 21 to 28 days. As you know, it takes an average of 21 days to start a new habit so these meal plans will make it much easier for you.

The third chapter is dedicated to the frequently asked questions about the Ketogenic Diet which are of course followed by their answers – again in simple, layman's terms.

Chapters four through eight are all filled with a total of fifty Ketogenic Diet recipes that are incorporated in the meal plans found in the second chapter. You will find recipes for Breakfast, Lunch, Snacks, Dinner, and even Desserts. Everything is practically "spoon-fed" to you, so to speak, in order to make your transition from a traditional, probably not so healthy, diet to the fat-burning, energy surging Ketogenic Diet.

It would also help you to know that the Ketogenic Diet has enabled people all over the world to achieve not just weight loss but also gain better health. In fact, it was originally designed as a therapeutic diet for children with epilepsy. Results reveal that those who follow the Ketogenic Diet experience at least fifty percent fewer seizures because of its neuro-protective benefits. Moreover, it is proven to contribute to the treatment of autoimmune disorders, including thyroid issues and type 1 diabetes.

The Ketogenic Diet has also helped many people overcome gluten insensitivity, Celiac Disease, the leaky gut syndrome, and other gastrointestinal issues. As it turns out, many of today's processed foods are full of irritants that slowly destroy our health and the best way to eliminate them from your system is by following this effective, albeit strict, diet.

For truth be told, the Ketogenic Diet is not going to be easy at first. This is because you must first have the guidance and consent of a licensed medical professional in order to find out your exact nutritional requirements. This is because the Ketogenic ratio for one person may be different compared to another, so what is considered as "one serving" for you might actually not be enough for someone else.

You must also be prepared to commit to the rules of the diet, and this includes completely eliminating carbohydrate-rich foods such as sugar and grains, both of which are highly common in the traditional Western diet.

On top of that, you must also be ready to invest in high quality sources of fat, which are relatively more costly than the readily available, pre-packaged foods on the market. For example, grass-fed butter is preferred over industrially produced butter that contains chemical additives. Likewise, free range eggs and pasture raised poultry, pork, and other meats are better options. The only way for the Ketogenic diet to be sustainable for you is when you have the budget ready for it.

Lastly, the Ketogenic Diet recommends that you prepare your own meals at home. By doing so, you are eliminating the contamination factor that is so common in foods prepared by strangers. This would also guarantee better nutritional value for your money, because you can invest in high quality ingredients without paying for someone else to cook them for you.

Hopefully all these precautions has not scared you away from starting the Ketogenic Diet, because our purpose is to help you set the right expectations before you begin. Nothing is more important than your health, and by starting the Ketogenic Diet and making it both sustainable and enjoyable, all the time, energy, and effort you put into planning and preparing your own meals, carefully choosing the best ingredients, and avoiding everything that is not good for you are well worth it. After all, the Ketogenic Diet is a fun, natural, and safe way to lose weight.

Even a study published in a 2003 issue of *The Journal of Clinical Endocrinology & Metabolism* revealed that those on the Ketogenic Diet lost over twice the amount of weight compared to those who followed a low fat, calorie restrictive diet. In addition, those who were on the Ketogenic diet had better improvements in their triglyceride and HDL cholesterol levels.

Another study, one published in the 2007 issue if *Diabetic Medicine*, discovered that those who followed the Ketogenic Diet lost thrice the amount of weight than those who were on the recommended diet of Diabetes UK.

There are plenty of other studies that can prove the highly promising weight loss effects of the Ketogenic Diet. However, the bottom-line is that you can only benefit from it if you apply it to your life. This is why we are so inspired to share the Ketogenic Diet with you in the form of this book.

Now, we are happy to invite you to go ahead and turn to the first chapter.

INTRODUCTION:

Did you know you can lose weight when you eat fat instead of carbs?

If that sounds crazy, then you probably have not heard about the Ketogenic Diet yet. This might sound like another fad, but the truth is this diet is over 80 years old and is proven to be highly effective!

In this book, you will learn the basic rules of the Ketogenic Diet, find answers to commonly asked questions about it, and most importantly, gain access to 7-day meal plans and fifty easy, delicious, and nutritious Keto-friendly recipes.

To find out find out more about the Ketogenic Diet, turn to chapter one right now. Because the sooner you start making the change, the sooner you can reach your goal weight.

CHAPTER 1: THE KETOGENIC DIET

It might sound completely insane to start a diet that is rich in fat, moderate in protein, and low in carbs in order to lose weight, but science has proven this to be highly effective. Of course, this does not mean you can indulge in oily foods and animal proteins all the time, because there are several highly important guidelines to strictly follow to avoid gaining even more weight or, worse, developing a cardiovascular disease while on the Keto diet.

In this chapter, you will learn the basics of the Keto diet and how it works. You will also get to know the rules to follow to safely and efficiently lose weight with the Keto diet.

WHAT IS THE KETO DIET?

The Ketogenic diet is the ultimate low carb, moderate protein, and high fat diet for weight loss. However, it was not originally designed to be so. Over eight decades ago, it was used as a mainstream of therapy to help treat epilepsy in children, but it was soon discovered that it conditions the body to burn fat instead of carbohydrates for energy. Therefore, those follow the Keto diet end up losing a significant amount of excess weight compared to those who eat high fat and high carb foods.

In addition, the Keto diet shows promising results in reducing the risk of the development of neurological disorders such as Alzheimer's disease and Parkinson's disease. While the specific reason for this is yet to be discovered in detail, the overall explanation shows that the central nervous system thrives in a diet that causes the body to use fat – not glucose – as its main energy source.

It is important to note, however, that weight loss and the other health benefits of the Keto diet would only take place once the body has transitioned from being glucose-dependent to being Keto-adapted – an effect that requires a minimum of 15 days of strictly following the Keto diet. Once you have become keto-adapted, you should stick to the Keto diet *for the rest of their life.* Otherwise, going back to a diet rich in carbs and fat will cause you to go back to being dependent on glucose, thus resulting to weight gain.

THE RULES TO FOLLOW

You should only start the Keto diet if your doctor or a licensed dietitian approves it. This is because not everyone is qualified to start the keto diet, especially if they have an existing medical condition or is taking prescription medication. Therefore, you should first get professional advice before attempting this diet.

Now, aside from getting your doctor or dietitian's approval, you should also be ready to commit to the rules of the Keto diet. Any deviance from the rules will instantly disrupt your path towards becoming keto-adapted.

So, to set your expectations, you should be prepared to commit to the following rules for the rest of your life:

Rule #1: You must completely avoid foods rich in carbohydrates, especially grains and sugar.

It is important to eliminate all rich sources of carbohydrates from your diet, especially if you are still on your way to becoming keto-adapted. Your body is considered to be "keto-adapted" once it starts to rely on fat as its main source of energy instead of glucose. This can only happen if the body is sufficiently deprived of carbs, because if there is enough carbs to break down to glucose and, in turn, convert to glycogen, your body would not have to resort to burning fat.

Once you have become keto-adapted and at the same time achieved the ideal healthy weight loss for your body type, you can slowly re-introduce healthy carbohydrates into your diet. However, it should amount to no more than 1 gram of carbohydrates per kilogram of your body weight. For instance, if you have reached your ideal body weight of 50 kilograms, then you should eat no more than 50 grams of carbs per day.

Rule #2: You should only choose to eat the best quality sources of natural fats.

The Keto diet promotes fat, but not just any kind of fat. Rather, it promotes the consumption of healthy fats, including those found in organic meat (grass-fed beef, free range pork, and wild game) and eggs, wild-caught fish and other seafood, organic dairy and cheese, dark chocolate, avocados, coconut and olive oils, yogurts, nuts, and seeds.

You must be prepared to allocate your food budget to these sources of fats, because low quality sources can put you at risk of developing heart disease. If you think you cannot sustainably purchase premium natural sources of healthy fats, then you are not likely to sustain the Keto diet for the rest of your life and should therefore consider other more cost-effective and healthy weight loss options, such as vegetarianism or veganism.

Rule #3: You must completely eliminate trans fat from your diet.

If there is one type of fat you need to avoid regardless of whether you are on the Keto diet or not, it is trans fat. Otherwise referred to as "trans fatty acids," trans fat is the main cause of increased LDL cholesterol levels, which in turn leads to the heightened risk of heart attacks and other cardiovascular diseases.

Trans fat is found in most industrially produced fats and oils, such as margarine and vegetable oil. Common examples of foods high in trans fat are baked goods such as cakes, cookies, crackers, pizza crusts, and pie crusts; packaged snacks such as corn chips, potato chips, and microwaveable popcorn; and deep-fried food, such as French fries, fried chicken, and donuts.

Aside from following these three main rules in the Keto diet, it is also important for you to exercise regularly in order to allow your body to burn your excess fat stores. The more energy your body expends every day, the faster you will become keto-adapted. To help you get started on the Keto diet, turn to the next chapter to learn more about how to plan Keto-friendly meals. Also, if you have other questions regarding the Keto diet, you may find the answers to them in Chapter 3.

CHAPTER 2: THE IDEAL 7-DAY KETO DIET PLAN

The purpose of a meal plan is more than just to ensure you are sticking to the rules of the Keto diet, for it is also meant to help you control your food budget and develop the right eating habits. It might take you some time to get used to preparing a meal plan once a week or – at the very least – twice a month, but once you do, you will realize how much easier your life is.

To help you get started on the Keto diet, we have devised four ideal 7-day meal plans for you using the recipes found in the succeeding chapters of this book.

Notice that the meal plans call for the same types of dishes every other day. The reason for this is to help minimize the cost and time you need to prepare your Keto-friendly meals. In other words, each recipe that calls for 4 servings, for example, literally means you will be preparing up to four meals. By doing this, you would only have to cook once for four days' worth of dinners, thus minimizing the effort you need to put into preparing your meals.

With all these in mind, you should not keep food for more than 3 days inside the refrigerator and you must never reheat the food more than once. Therefore, if you are cooking for yourself, then you can halve the recipe measurements, if you like, so that you can only cook one meal for immediate serving, and another for reheating the following day or two days from the time you cooked it.

Lastly, notice that the meal plans recommend at least 5 meals: breakfast, morning snack, lunch, afternoon snack, dinner, and the optional dessert. This is because eating five meals a day will prevent you from getting unhealthy cravings for the high-carb food your body was used to before you started the Keto diet.

The idea is to be one step ahead of your cravings by having carefully prepared food ready and by sticking to a solid meal schedule. Try to have eat every 3 to 4 hours throughout your waking day. For instance, if you tend to wake up at 7 in the morning, then you should have breakfast on or before 7:30. Then, at 10:30 am, you should have your morning snack. At 1:30 pm, you can have your lunch. After that, 4:30 pm is your afternoon snack time. Dinner should be ready by 7:30 pm, followed by a dessert, if you wish.

All in all, you need to remember the following guidelines when it comes to planning meals for the Keto diet:

- **Plan your meals ahead, at least once a week.**
- **Cook in bulk to save time, energy, and money.**
- **Store prepared meals up to 3 days in the refrigerator; reheat only once.**
- **Eat five small meals per day.**
- **Maintain fixed meal times with each meal spaced 3 to 4 hours apart.**

MEAL PLAN 1

Day 1

Breakfast: CREAMY SPINACH SCRAMBLE

Snack: CHEESY FRIED AVOCADO STICKS

Lunch: STIR-FRIED BEEF WITH MUSHROOMS AND BROCCOLI

Snack: CHEESY FRIED AVOCADO STICKS

Dinner: BEEF STROGANOFF

Dessert (optional): CREAMY CHOCO COCONUT CREAM

Day 2

Breakfast: KETO MINI QUICHE LORRAINE

Snack: CHEESY FRIED AVOCADO STICKS

Lunch: MAC-CAULIFLOWER 'N' CHEESE

Snack: CHEESY FRIED AVOCADO STICKS

Dinner: CHEESY CHICKEN THIGHS STUFFED WITH KALE AND BACON

Dessert (optional): STRAWBERRY COCONUT CREAM POPS

Day 3

Breakfast: CREAMY SPINACH SCRAMBLE

Snack: CHEESY CAULIFLOWER BITES

Lunch: STIR-FRIED BEEF WITH MUSHROOMS AND BROCCOLI

Snack: CHEESY CAULIFLOWER BITES

Dinner: BEEF STROGANOFF

Dessert (optional): CREAMY CHOCO COCONUT CREAM

Day 4

Breakfast: KETO MINI QUICHE LORRAINE

Snack: CHEESY CAULIFLOWER BITES

Lunch: MAC-CAULIFLOWER 'N' CHEESE

Snack: CHEESY CAULIFLOWER BITES

Dinner: CHEESY CHICKEN THIGHS STUFFED WITH KALE AND BACON

Dessert (optional): STRAWBERRY COCONUT CREAM POPS

Day 5

Breakfast: BLACKBERRY ALMOND MUFFINS

Snack: BARBEQUE TOFU FRIES

Lunch: BRAISED STUFFED PORK CHOPS IN MUSHROOM SAUCE

Snack: BARBEQUE TOFU FRIES

Dinner: PROVENCAL BEEF STEW

Dessert (optional): BUTTER DARK CHOCOLATE BROWNIES

Day 6

Breakfast: BAKED CHEESY EGG AVOCADO CUPS

Snack: BARBEQUE TOFU FRIES

Lunch: BRAISED STUFFED PORK CHOPS IN MUSHROOM SAUCE

Snack: BARBEQUE TOFU FRIES

Dinner: CHICKEN AVOCADO LETTUCE WRAPS

Dessert (optional): BUTTER PECAN BITES

Day 7

Breakfast: BLACKBERRY ALMOND MUFFINS

Snack: CAJUN TRAIL MIX

Lunch: GRILLED SEAFOOD AND AVOCADO SALAD

Snack: CAJUN TRAIL MIX

Dinner: PROVENCAL BEEF STEW

Dessert (optional): BUTTER DARK CHOCOLATE BROWNIES

MEAL PLAN 2

Day 1

Breakfast: BAKED CHEESY EGG AVOCADO CUPS

Snack: CAJUN TRAIL MIX

Lunch: ASIAN CHICKEN SALAD

Snack: CAJUN TRAIL MIX

Dinner: CHICKEN AVOCADO LETTUCE WRAPS

Dessert (optional): CRISPY CHOCOLATE-COATED BACON

Day 2

Breakfast: HAM AND BROCCOLI MINI QUICHE

Snack: CHEESY ARTICHOKE AND SPINACH SPREAD

Lunch: GRILLED SEAFOOD AND AVOCADO SALAD

Snack: CHEESY ARTICHOKE AND SPINACH SPREAD

Dinner: HERB, SCALLION, AND MUSHROOM STUFFED LAMB CHOPS

Dessert (optional): BUTTER PECAN BITES

Day 3

Breakfast: SUNNY SIDE UP EGGS OVER BACON-WRAPPED ASPARAGUS SPEARS

Snack: CHEESY ARTICHOKE AND SPINACH SPREAD

Lunch: ASIAN CHICKEN SALAD

Snack: CHEESY ARTICHOKE AND SPINACH SPREAD

Dinner: CHICKEN CHILI

Dessert (optional): CRISPY CHOCOLATE-COATED BACON

Day 4

Breakfast: HAM AND BROCCOLI MINI QUICHE

Snack: SAVORY SPINACH STUFFED MUSHROOMS

Lunch: SQUASH SPAGHETTI WITH MEATBALLS

Snack: SAVORY SPINACH STUFFED MUSHROOMS

Dinner: HERB, SCALLION, AND MUSHROOM STUFFED LAMB CHOPS

Dessert (optional): MINI RASPBERRY CREAM CHEESE BALLS

Day 5

Breakfast: SUNNY SIDE UP EGGS OVER BACON-WRAPPED ASPARAGUS SPEARS

Snack: SAVORY SPINACH STUFFED MUSHROOMS

Lunch: HERBED CREAMY CHEESE PORK CHOPS

Snack: SAVORY SPINACH STUFFED MUSHROOMS

Dinner: CHICKEN CHILI

Dessert (optional): KETO COFFEE CHOCOLATE CHIP COOKIES

Day 6

Breakfast: PUMPKIN AND CREAM CHEESE PANCAKES

Snack: SAVORY KALE CHIPS

Lunch: SQUASH SPAGHETTI WITH MEATBALLS

Snack: SAVORY KALE CHIPS

Dinner: MEDITERRANEAN SEAFOOD, SAUSAGE AND PEPPER STEW

Dessert (optional): MINI RASPBERRY CREAM CHEESE BALLS

Day 7

Breakfast: CHEDDAR CHEESE AND BROCCOLI MINI QUICHES

Snack: SAVORY KALE CHIPS

Lunch: HERBED CREAMY CHEESE PORK CHOPS

Snack: SAVORY KALE CHIPS

Dinner: THAI-INSPIRED BROILED CHICKEN SKEWERS

Dessert (optional): KETO COFFEE CHOCOLATE CHIP COOKIES

MEAL PLAN 3

Day 1

Breakfast: PUMPKIN AND CREAM CHEESE PANCAKES

Snack: SOUTHWESTERN STUFFED EGGS

Lunch: ASIAN-INSPIRED TUNA WITH CAULIFLOWER RICE

Snack: SOUTHWESTERN STUFFED EGGS

Dinner: MEDITERRANEAN SEAFOOD, SAUSAGE AND PEPPER STEW

Dessert (optional): COCONUT LIME BUTTER BALLS

Day 2

Breakfast: CHEDDAR CHEESE AND BROCCOLI MINI QUICHES

Snack: SOUTHWESTERN STUFFED EGGS

Lunch: CLASSIC PORK STEW

Snack: SOUTHWESTERN STUFFED EGGS

Dinner: THAI-INSPIRED BROILED CHICKEN SKEWERS

Dessert (optional): KETO GINGERSNAPS

Day 3

Breakfast: CHEESY EGG AND BACON KETO MUFFINS

Snack: COCONUT BERRY SHAKE

Lunch: ASIAN-INSPIRED TUNA WITH CAULIFLOWER RICE

Snack: COCONUT BERRY SHAKE

Dinner: BEEF TACO SALAD WRAPS

Dessert (optional): COCONUT LIME BUTTER BALLS

Day 4

Breakfast: GRUYERE, GARLIC AND BASIL SCRAMBLED EGGS

Snack: COCONUT BERRY SHAKE

Lunch: CLASSIC PORK STEW

Snack: COCONUT BERRY SHAKE

Dinner: OVEN-ROASTED BUTTER GARLIC HADDOCK WITH SWISS CHARD

Dessert (optional): KETO GINGERSNAPS

Day 5

Breakfast: CHEESY EGG AND BACON KETO MUFFINS

Snack: SPICY GUACAMOLE WITH BACON BITS

Lunch: VEGGIE BEEF LASAGNA

Snack: SPICY GUACAMOLE WITH BACON BITS

Dinner: BEEF TACO SALAD WRAPS

Dessert (optional): KETO GINGERSNAPS

Day 6

Breakfast: GRUYERE, GARLIC AND BASIL SCRAMBLED EGGS

Snack: SPICY GUACAMOLE WITH BACON BITS

Lunch: STIR-FRIED BEEF WITH MUSHROOMS AND BROCCOLI

Snack: SPICY GUACAMOLE WITH BACON BITS

Dinner: OVEN-ROASTED BUTTER GARLIC HADDOCK WITH SWISS CHARD

Dessert (optional): PEANUT BUTTER AND CREAM CHEESE CHEWIES

Day 7

Breakfast: KETO MINI QUICHE LORRAINE

Snack: CHEESY FRIED AVOCADO STICKS

Lunch: VEGGIE BEEF LASAGNA

Snack: CHEESY FRIED AVOCADO STICKS

Dinner: BEEF STROGANOFF

Dessert (optional): CREAMY CHOCO COCONUT CREAM

MEAL PLAN 4

Day 1

Breakfast: BLACKBERRY ALMOND MUFFINS

Snack: CHEESY FRIED AVOCADO STICKS

Lunch: STIR-FRIED BEEF WITH MUSHROOMS AND BROCCOLI

Snack: CHEESY FRIED AVOCADO STICKS

Dinner: CHEESY CHICKEN THIGHS STUFFED WITH KALE AND BACON

Dessert (optional): PEANUT BUTTER AND CREAM CHEESE CHEWIES

Day 2

Breakfast: KETO MINI QUICHE LORRAINE

Snack: CHEESY CAULIFLOWER BITES

Lunch: MAC-CAULIFLOWER 'N' CHEESE

Snack: CHEESY CAULIFLOWER BITES

Dinner: BEEF STROGANOFF

Dessert (optional): CREAMY CHOCO COCONUT CREAM

Day 3

Breakfast: BLACKBERRY ALMOND MUFFINS

Snack: CHEESY CAULIFLOWER BITES

Lunch: BRAISED STUFFED PORK CHOPS IN MUSHROOM SAUCE

Snack: CHEESY CAULIFLOWER BITES

Dinner: CHEESY CHICKEN THIGHS STUFFED WITH KALE AND BACON

Dessert (optional): STRAWBERRY COCONUT CREAM POPS

Day 4

Breakfast: BAKED CHEESY EGG AVOCADO CUPS

Snack: BARBEQUE TOFU FRIES

Lunch: MAC-CAULIFLOWER 'N' CHEESE

Snack: BARBEQUE TOFU FRIES

Dinner: PROVENCAL BEEF STEW

Dessert (optional): BUTTER DARK CHOCOLATE BROWNIES

Day 5

Breakfast: HAM AND BROCCOLI MINI QUICHE

Snack: BARBEQUE TOFU FRIES

Lunch: BRAISED STUFFED PORK CHOPS IN MUSHROOM SAUCE

Snack: BARBEQUE TOFU FRIES

Dinner: CHICKEN AVOCADO LETTUCE WRAPS

Dessert (optional): STRAWBERRY COCONUT CREAM POPS

Day 6

Breakfast: BAKED CHEESY EGG AVOCADO CUPS

Snack: CAJUN TRAIL MIX

Lunch: GRILLED SEAFOOD AND AVOCADO SALAD

Snack: CAJUN TRAIL MIX

Dinner: PROVENCAL BEEF STEW

Dessert (optional): BUTTER DARK CHOCOLATE BROWNIES

Day 7

Breakfast: HAM AND BROCCOLI MINI QUICHE

Snack: CAJUN TRAIL MIX

Lunch: ASIAN CHICKEN SALAD

Snack: CAJUN TRAIL MIX

Dinner: CHICKEN AVOCADO LETTUCE WRAPS

Dessert (optional): BUTTER PECAN BITES

CHAPTER 3: FREQUENTLY ASKED QUESTIONS

Q: How does the Keto diet cause you to lose weight?

A: Maintaining the Keto diet for at least 14 days will cause your liver to produce ketones, an organic compound that causes your body to start burning fat for energy instead of glucose, or the basic form of carbohydrates in the body. However, it is important to note that eating Keto-friendly meals alone will cause you to lose weight. You must remember to avoid **all** carbohydrate-rich foods and to start exercising regularly to boost your metabolism as well.

Q: Will going on the Keto diet increase my risk of getting a heart attack?

A: Saturated fatty acids in animal fats have been receiving a lot of flak as they are said to be linked to heart disease. However, an increasing amount of research reveals that trans fat – not saturated fatty acids – are directly linked to cardiovascular diseases. Trans fats are found in processed food such as margarine spreads and vegetable oils, therefore they should be eliminated. The rule of thumb is to avoid all processed, unnatural fats (especially those with the word "hydrogenated" found in their ingredients list) and to focus on eating the ones found in nature, such as fats from grass-fed, pasture-raised beef, organic pork, chicken, and eggs, wild-caught seafood, and of course, nuts and seeds.

Q: What makes the Keto diet more effective than other weight loss diets?

A: The Keto diet is extremely low in carbohydrates, and since excessive carb consumption – not fat consumption – is the cause of obesity, significantly reducing carbs will naturally lead to weight loss. Another reason why the Keto diet can help one lose weight more effectively is that it does not support food deprivation. People who go on extremely calorie diets often up binge-eating afterwards. However, those who are on a sustainable Keto diet continue to lose weight without losing muscle mass and without ending up binge eating.

Q: Do I need a licensed dietitian's approval to start the Keto diet?

A: Yes, you definitely need the guidance and support of a licensed dietitian before you start *any* kind of weight loss program. The Keto diet, in particular, requires you to monitor and measure your ketone levels at least once a week until you become keto-adapted. In addition, not all people are candidates for the Keto diet. If you have a specific medical condition such as type 2 diabetes or atherosclerosis, or if you are currently on prescription medication, you absolutely must consult a doctor before you try any Keto-friendly meals.

Q: Isn't a diet high in fat, like the Keto diet, dangerous to health?

A: A diet high in fat is only potentially life-threatening if it is also **high in carbohydrates**. This is because the body will still continue to rely on the glucose from the carb-filled foods for energy and any fat consumed is stored. This would naturally elevate one's bad cholesterol levels, leading to the development of atherosclerosis and other heart diseases.

However, the Keto diet is high in fat **but extremely low in carbohydrates.** So; by significantly reduce carbohydrates from your diet and replace it instead with fat, your body will adapt to this change by resorting to fat as its source of energy.

Q: Can a person on the Keto diet have a carbohydrate "cheat day?"

A: The simple answer is No. While there is such a thing as "cyclic ketogenic dieting," or following the keto diet strictly for 5 days and then eating regular carb-filled meals for 2 days, studies note that those who apply this tend to lose lean muscle mass, which you definitely do not want to happen. Moreover, you will end up gaining even more weight if you eat carb-filled food soon after following the keto diet, because your body has not entered the ketosis yet when you start reintroducing carbs into it. The better thing to do would be to stick to a strict keto diet for at least 21 days, then very slowly reintroduce **small** amounts of carbs every day, or about 1 gram of carbs per kilogram of your keto-adapted body weight.

Q: Do I have to count calories when on the Keto diet?

A: In a perfect world, people count the calories they consume every day in order to ensure that they are not going beyond their daily requirements. However, in reality people have roughly different requirements depending on how they would expend their energy that day. In addition, specific issues such as endocrine or metabolic disorders have a tremendous effect on a person's daily caloric needs. It is therefore wiser to focus on eating healthy and to exercise regularly than to strictly monitor the amount of calories you consume. In the Keto diet, you should be mindful of your food choices so that you can ensure you are only eating high fat, moderate protein, and low or no carb meals every time. It is also important not to overeat even if the food is Keto-friendly, because you still need to eat less than what your body requires so that it would resort to burning its excess fat stores.

Q: Is it possible to over-consume fat in the Keto diet?

A: While eating fat and protein will make you feel satiated for a longer period of time than carbs, it is still important to remember that fat contains 9 calories per gram versus 4 calories per gram in protein or carbs. Therefore, it is definitely possible to overindulge in fatty food, even if you are on the Keto diet. To avoid overeating fat, you can use an online keto calculator to determine the maximum amount of fat in grams or calories you can eat per day.

Q: How do you know that you have entered Ketosis?

A: The most accurate way to tell if you have entered ketosis is by getting a urinalysis or a blood ketone meter. In the latter, you can tell that you are in light ketosis if the result shows 0.5 to 0.8 mmol/L; medium ketosis if it is 0.9 to 1.4 mmol/L; or deep ketosis if it is 1.5 to 3.0 mmol/L. It is also important to note that ketosis triggers headaches, lethargy, constipation, and the frequent urge to urinate. This is completely normal and the best ways to cope with the symptoms are by drinking plenty of water; eating low-carb, high fiber vegetables; incorporating psyllium fiber, chia seeds, and/or flax seeds into the diet; and taking a magnesium supplement.

CHAPTER 4: KETO BREAKFAST RECIPES

In its simplest form, the Keto-friendly breakfast consists of a plateful of scrambled eggs with avocado and leafy greens, a side of crisp bacon, and a mug of black coffee or green tea. Of course, variety is key to keep meals interesting, especially when it comes to breakfast. So, whenever you are in the mood to change things up you should choose any of the following recipes for a healthy, hearty, and satisfying breakfast.

Creamy Spinach Scramble

Scrambled eggs are tasty enough on their own, but if you add some butter, cream, and plenty of spinach, it becomes heavenly. This recipe shows you how to create an easy, tasty, and extremely healthy hearty breakfast.

Number of Servings: 4

You will Need:

- **12 large organic eggs**
- **1 onion, peeled and minced**
- **2 cups chopped spinach**
- **1 cup heavy cream**
- **2 Tbsp. grass-fed butter**
- **Sea salt, to taste**
- **Freshly ground black pepper, to taste**

How to Prepare:

Break the eggs into a large bowl and whisk well until frothy. Add the heavy cream with a pinch of salt and pepper. Mix again to combine.

Place a frying pan over medium flame and heat through. Once hot, add the butter and swirl to coat. Stir in the onion and sauté until translucent.

Add the egg mixture and scrape across the pan, tilting the pan to cook the runny sides. Continue to scramble until the eggs are cooked to a desired consistency – fluffy, light, and still slightly moist.

Transfer to a serving plate and serve right away.

Nutritional Information per Serving

Calories: 320

Fat: 32 g

Protein: 15 g

Carbohydrates: 3 g

Fiber: 32 g

KETO MINI QUICHE LORRAINE

Bacon with heavy cream is best served in the morning, whether for breakfast or brunch, because they are so full of filling protein. If you want to make this recipe ahead, you should double it and use a regular pie pan instead of a mini one so that you can refrigerate the extra slices to be reheated for the rest of the week. That said, this mini quiche Lorraine is not for those who don't love cheese, because it is filled with two of the most popular cheeses on the planet: Swiss and Gruyere. Enjoy on special mornings or in mornings when you want to feel extra special.

Number of Servings: 4

You will Need:

- ½ lb. thick, organic, pasture-raised bacon strips
- 2 large organic eggs
- 2 garlic cloves, peeled and minced
- 1 large white onion, peeled and minced
- ¾ cup heavy cream
- ½ cup shredded Swiss cheese
- ¼ cup shredded Gruyere cheese
- Sea salt, to taste
- Freshly ground black pepper, to taste
- Coconut oil cooking spray, as needed

How to Prepare:

Set the oven to 350 degrees F to preheat. Place the oven rack in the center section of the oven. Lightly coat a mini pie pan with the coconut oil cooking spray and set aside.

Place a large frying pan over medium high flame and heat through.

Once hot, add the bacon and cook for about 4 minutes per side, or until crisp and golden brown. Transfer the bacon strips on a plate lined with paper towels and set aside.

Reduce the flame to medium low under the same frying pan with the bacon fat still in it. Stir in the onion and sauté until translucent for about 3 minutes. Then, add the garlic and sauté until fragrant, about 30 seconds.

Transfer the onion and garlic into a bowl using a slotted spoon and set aside. Drain the bacon fat and wipe the frying pan clean.

Break the eggs open into a mixing bowl and add the heavy cream. Whisk well until smooth and creamy. Fold in the Swiss and Gruyere cheeses with a pinch of salt and pepper. Then, chop the cooled bacon strips and fold them into the egg and heavy cream mixture as well, followed by the onion and garlic mixture. Mix everything well.

Pour the mixture into the prepared mini pie pan. Place the pan inside the preheated oven and bake for 15 to 20 minutes, or until the quiche Lorraine is cooked through and firm.

Transfer the pan to a cooling rack and let stand for about 5 minutes. Slice and serve while still warm.

Nutritional Information per Serving

Calories: 498

Fat: 42.7 g

Protein: 22.1 g

Carbohydrates: 2.3 g

Fiber: 0 g

BLACKBERRY ALMOND MUFFINS

Breakfast muffins should not be crossed out of your list just because you are on the Keto diet. This recipe combines the succulence of blackberries and the classic taste of almonds to give you comfortingly delicious and fluffy muffins in the morning. Serve with a pat of butter or a dollop of cream cheese on top.

Number of Servings: 4 (3 muffins per serving)

You will Need:

- 2 large organic eggs
- 4 oz. fresh or frozen blackberries
- 3 cups almond flour
- 2 cups almond milk
- ¼ cup toasted unsweetened shredded coconut flakes
- 1 Tbsp. stevia
- 1 tsp. nutmeg
- 1 tsp. baking powder
- 1 tsp. sea salt
- Coconut oil cooking spray, as needed

How to Prepare:

Set the oven to 400 degrees F to preheat. Lightly coat 12 muffin molds with coconut oil cooking spray. Set aside.

In a bowl, combine the almond flour, stevia, nutmeg, baking powder, and sea salt. Set aside.

In another bowl, whisk the eggs and then add the almond milk. Mix well to combine.

Gradually combine the flour mixture with the egg mixture until combined. Do not over-mix. Fold in the shredded coconut flakes and mix until thoroughly incorporated.

Pour the batter into the muffin molds, then divide the blackberries among the muffin servings.

Bake for 10 minutes. After that, reduce to 300 degrees F and bake again for an additional 10 minutes, or until the muffins are golden brown and puffed. Insert a toothpick into the center of one muffin; if it comes out clean, it is ready.

Place the muffins on a cooling rack and let stand for 5 minutes before serving. Best served warm. Store leftover muffins in the freezer for up to 3 months; reheat before serving.

Nutritional Information per Serving

Calories: 531

Fat: 63 g

Protein: 39 g

Carbohydrates: 15 g

Fiber: 15 g

BAKED CHEESY EGG AVOCADO CUPS

Avocados are arguably the Keto crowd favorite of all the fruits, mainly because it is so rich in healthy fats! Eating an avocado half will keep you full for a much longer time than any other fruit will, plus it will nourish your body with plenty of Vitamins C and B6. Add some cheese and egg on top and you are in Keto breakfast heaven!

Number of Servings: 4

You will Need:

- **2 large avocados**
- **4 organic eggs**
- **6 Tbsp. shredded Colby cheese**
- **1 Tbsp. freshly squeezed lemon juice**
- **Sea salt, to taste**
- **Freshly ground black pepper, to taste**

How to Prepare:

Set the oven to 475 degrees F to preheat.

Evenly slice each avocado in half and discard the stone. Then, carefully scoop out just enough of the inside of the center of each avocado to create a "bowl" large enough for one egg.

Place each avocado half, open-faced side up, into a ramekin to keep them secured. Sprinkle the freshly squeezed lemon juice over each half. Set aside.

Carefully crack an egg open, separating the yolk from the whites.

Slide one yolk into the prepared avocado half and then pour its white over it. Repeat with the remaining eggs and avocado halves. Season everything lightly with salt and pepper.

Top each prepared avocado and egg serving with the shredded Colby cheese. Bake for 15 minutes, or until the eggs are cooked to a desired level of consistency.

Transfer to a cooling rack and let stand for about 5 minutes. Best served warm.

Nutritional Information per Serving

Calories: 324

Fat: 28.5 g

Protein: 10.8 g

Carbohydrates: 2.7 g

Fiber: 6.8 g

HAM AND BROCCOLI MINI QUICHE

Wake up to a healthy and filling breakfast with this Keto twist of the classic quiche. If you love the taste of this breakfast dish as much as everyone else does, you should consider doubling or even tripling the recipe. That way, you can just store them in the refrigerator for easy reheating and eating on busy mornings.

Number of Servings: 4

You will Need:

- **4 organic eggs**
- **¾ cup sliced organic smoked ham**
- **¾ cup finely chopped broccoli florets**
- **½ cup heavy cream**
- **½ cup Cheddar cheese**
- **1 Tbsp. olive oil**
- **½ tsp. red chili flakes**
- **Olive oil cooking spray, as needed**

How to Prepare:

Set the oven to 350 degrees F to preheat. Lightly coat a mini pie or quiche pan with the olive oil cooking spray and set aside.

In a large bowl, break open the eggs and then whisk well. Pour in the heavy cream and sprinkle in the red chili flakes. Blend until thoroughly combined.

Layer the sliced ham in the bottom of the pan and then layer the chopped broccoli florets on top. Sprinkle the Cheddar cheese on top of everything.

Pour the egg mixture on top. Bake for 8 to 10 minutes, or until fluffy and golden brown. Transfer to a cooling rack and let stand for 5 minutes before slicing and serving. Best served warm.

Nutritional Information per Serving

Calories: 380

Fat: 28 g

Protein: 12 g

Carbohydrates: 4 g

Fiber: 6 g

SUNNY SIDE UP EGGS OVER BACON-WRAPPED ASPARAGUS SPEARS

This sumptuous dish makes for a pretty picture on the breakfast table, and the delicious blend of flavor and texture are just the cherry (or should we say, sunny side egg?) on top. You can enjoy this breakfast right before a particularly busy day, because it is packed full of energy and protein. Also, make sure the asparagus is just crunchy enough to bite and the eggs cooked over easy for a sinfully smooth mouthful. To make it even more delectable, add a generous spoonful of cream cheese or sour cream.

Number of Servings: 4

You will Need:

- 24 asparagus spears, trimmed
- 8 organic eggs
- 4 organic strips of bacon
- 1 garlic clove, peeled and minced
- 2 Tbsp. grass-fed butter
- 1 tsp. onion powder
- Sea salt, to taste
- Freshly ground black pepper, to taste

How to Prepare:

Set the oven to 400 degrees F to preheat.

Meanwhile, divide the asparagus spears into 8 bundles (3 spears per bundle). Then, slice the bacon strips in half and then wrap each half around one bundle of asparagus spears. Secure with toothpicks and arrange on the prepared baking sheet in a single layer.

Sprinkle the minced garlic over the bacon-wrapped asparagus, followed by the onion powder and some salt and pepper.

Transfer the baking sheet with the bacon-wrapped asparagus into the preheated oven and bake for 10 minutes, or until the bacon is crisp and cooked through.

While waiting for the asparagus spears, place a large frying pan over medium high flame and melt a quarter of the butter. Swirl to coat the base of the pan. Then, break 2 eggs into the hot butter, taking care not to break the yolks.

Cook the sunny-side up eggs to a desired level of consistency and season lightly with salt and pepper. Transfer to a plate. Repeat with the remaining butter and eggs.

Once the bacon-wrapped asparagus are done, divide them into four servings and top with two sunny side up eggs each. Best served right away.

Nutritional Information per Serving

Calories: 479

Fat: 35.5 g

Protein: 32.9 g

Carbohydrates: 5.1 g

Fiber: 3.2 g

PUMPKIN AND CREAM CHEESE PANCAKES

These pancakes will remind you of a slice of velvety pumpkin pie, except they are significantly lower in carbs and higher in flavor, creaminess, and protein. So say goodbye to those unhealthy, empty calorie pancake mixtures and give this one a try instead.

Number of Servings: 4

You will Need:

- 1 large organic egg
- ½ cup steamed organic pumpkin
- ½ cup cream cheese
- 1/3 cup coconut flour
- 2 Tbsp. melted grass-fed butter
- ¼ tsp. nutmeg
- ¼ tsp. pumpkin spice
- ½ tsp. stevia
- Coconut oil cooking spray, as needed

How to Prepare:

Combine the steamed pumpkin, coconut flour, cream cheese, pumpkin spice, stevia, nutmeg, melted butter, and eggs in a food processor. Cover and mix well until evenly combined.

Transfer the batter into a bowl and cover. Refrigerate for 15 minutes.

Coat a pancake griddle with the coconut oil cooking spray. Place over medium flame and heat through. Once hot, reduce to low flame.

Take the batter out of the refrigerator. Ladle into the pancake griddle and cook for 2 minutes per side, or until fluffy and golden brown. Transfer to a plate and cover to keep warm.

Repeat with the remaining batter. Divide into four servings and serve right away. Best served with a pat of butter or a dollop of cream cheese.

Nutritional Information per Serving

Calories: 150

Fat: 22 g

Protein: 10 g

Carbohydrates: 5 g

Fiber: 2 g

CHEDDAR CHEESE AND BROCCOLI MINI QUICHES

Broccoli and cheddar cheese go so well together, it is not a wonder that these mini quiches is a favorite breakfast dish even among those who do not particularly like this cruciferous vegetable. These muffins are best served with a side of sliced low-carb veggies such as cucumbers to help spread the sharpness of the cheese.

Number of Servings: 4

You will Need:

- 5 large organic eggs
- 1 garlic clove, peeled and minced
- 1 ½ cups chopped broccoli florets
- ¾ cup shredded sharp Cheddar cheese
- ¾ cup heavy cream
- Sea salt, to taste
- Freshly ground black pepper, to taste
- Coconut oil cooking spray, as needed

How to Prepare:

Set the oven to 350 degrees F to preheat.

Lightly coat four ramekins with coconut oil cooking spray and arrange them on a baking pan. Set aside.

Fill a small pot with water and add a pinch of salt. Cover and place over high flame to bring to a boil. Once boiling, turn off the heat and add the broccoli florets. Blanch for no more than 15 seconds. Immediately drain the broccoli and place in a colander to drain. Set aside.

Break the eggs open into a mixing bowl and add the heavy cream with a pinch of salt and pepper. Whisk until smooth and creamy.

Add the minced garlic, shredded Cheddar cheese, and blanched broccoli to the egg mixture then mix well until evenly combined.

Divide the mixture evenly among the prepared ramekins and then place the baking pan into the preheated oven. Bake for 30 minutes, or until golden brown and fluffy.

Carefully transfer the ramekins onto a cooling rack and allow to set for about 5 minutes. Best served warm.

Nutritional Information per Serving

Calories: 255

Fat: 21.1 g

Protein: 13.7 g

Carbohydrates: 2.7 g

Fiber: 0.9 g

CHEESY EGG AND BACON KETO MUFFINS

These scrumptious bite-sized meals are more than just a mere mouthful, because they are packed with enough protein and savory flavor to get you pumped up for a busy morning routine.

It would be a great idea to double up the recipe to make these ahead, then freeze them and reheat in the microwave oven whenever you want.

Number of Servings: 4

You will Need:

- **6 large strips of organic, pasture-raised bacon**
- **4 large organic eggs**
- **½ cup heavy cream**
- **½ cup shredded Monterey Jack cheese**
- **Sea salt, to taste**
- **Freshly ground black pepper, to taste**

How to Prepare:

Set the oven to 350 degrees F to preheat.

Take one strip of bacon and then wrap it around the inner edges of a muffin mold to create a "wall" for your keto muffins. Do the same with three more bacon strips.

Slice the remaining two bacon strips into four equal pieces. Divide them among the four prepared muffin molds and place them in the bottom to create a base for the keto muffins. Set aside.

Break the eggs into a bowl and add the heavy cream. Season lightly with salt and pepper and then beat well until smooth and creamy.

Divide the egg and heavy cream mixture among the prepared muffin cups. Then, divide the shredded Monterey Jack cheese evenly among them.

Put the prepared muffin molds into the preheated oven and bake for 30 minutes or until golden brown.

Place on a cooling rack and allow to cool for 5 minutes before serving. Best served warm.

Nutritional Information per Serving

Calories: 359

Fat: 29 g

Protein: 22.5 g

Carbohydrates: 1.5 g

Fiber: 0 g

GRUYERE, GARLIC AND BASIL SCRAMBLED EGGS

Here is another take on the scrambled eggs dish. This time, it has got the smooth, and creamy Gruyere cheese in it, along with fresh basil and garlic, as well as a little bit of heavy cream. It is best complemented with a fresh green and red pepper salad and perhaps a hot cup of black or buttered coffee.

Number of Servings: 4

You will Need:

- 8 large organic eggs
- 4 garlic cloves, peeled and crushed
- 4 Tbsp. water
- 4 Tbsp. chopped fresh basil
- 4 Tbsp. freshly grated Gruyere cheese
- 2 Tbsp. heavy cream
- 4 tsp. olive oil

How to Prepare:

Break the eggs open into a large bowl and then add the water, heavy cream, basil, and grated Gruyere cheese. Whisk vigorously until smooth. Set aside.

Place a large frying pan over low flame and add the olive oil. Swirl to coat.

Stir in the crushed garlic and sauté until fragrant and pale golden brown; take care not to burn them.

Whisk the egg mixture one more time and then pour it into the skillet, over the garlic. Scramble until fluffy and tender, but still slightly moist, if desired.

Divide the scrambled eggs into four servings and serve right away.

Nutritional Information per Serving

Calories: 237

Fat: 18 g

Protein: 15 g

Carbohydrates: 3 g

Fiber: 0 g

CHAPTER 5: KETO LUNCH RECIPES

Lunch time can get really hectic, especially during the weekday. So much so that people often turn to eating fast foods and other convenient but extremely unhealthy meal options. However, it is important to stick to the Keto diet rules no matter how busy you are, so preparation and planning are key. You can make your lunch meals ahead of time easily just as long as you have a refrigerator in which to store them and a microwave in which to reheat them. Also, with the help of these lunch recipes, you will never run out of ideas on what to put into your lunchbox. Enjoy!

STIR-FRIED BEEF WITH MUSHROOMS AND BROCCOLI

Lunch becomes much easier when everything you need can be cooked in one wok. This particular recipe makes use of the traditional Asian flavors of soy sauce, sesame oil, and ginger to bring out the tastiness of beef, mushrooms, and broccoli. Also, if you want to add more fiber and nutrients, you can double the amount of broccoli in each serving.

Number of Servings: 4

You will Need:

- 4 cups thinly sliced organic, grass-fed sirloin or tenderloin
- 1 large yellow onion, peeled and diced
- 1 red bell pepper, cored, seeded, and sliced into thin strips
- 2 garlic cloves, peeled and minced
- 2 cups finely sliced broccoli florets
- 2 cups chopped mushrooms
- 1 cup chopped and trimmed string beans
- ¼ cup sesame oil
- 6 Tbsp. freshly minced ginger
- 4 Tbsp. soy sauce
- 4 Tbsp. rice vinegar
- 4 Tbsp. tomato sauce

How to Prepare:

Place a large wok over high flame and heat through. Once hot, add half the sesame oil and reduce to medium low flame.

Add the beef, onion, and bell pepper and stir fry until the beef is halfway cooked.

Add the ginger and garlic for and sauté 30 seconds, or until fragrant. Then, stir in the broccoli, string beans, and mushrooms. Increase to high flame and stir fry for about 10 minutes, or until everything is tender.

Add the soy sauce, vinegar, and tomato sauce. Mix well until the beef is cooked through and tender.

Transfer to a serving platter and serve right away. Store any leftovers in an airtight container and refrigerate for up to 3 days. Reheat before serving.

Nutritional Information per Serving

Calories: 200

Fat: 22 g

Protein: 13 g

Carbohydrates: 5.5 g

Fiber: 3 g

MAC-CAULIFLOWER 'N' CHEESE

When it comes to replacing carb-filled ingredients such as pasta and pizza crusts, cauliflower is your go-to vegetable. Not only is it Keto friendly, but it is also rich in vitamins B6, C and K, riboflavin, magnesium, fiber, and protein, to name a few. If you are not fond of cauliflower, then this creamy, cheesy cauliflower mac 'n' cheese recipe will definitely change your mind and kick your pasta cravings to the curb.

Number of Servings: 4

You will Need:

- **1 small garlic clove, peeled and minced**
- **2 cups chopped cauliflower florets**
- **½ cup heavy cream**
- **½ cup shredded Cheddar cheese**
- **¼ cup shredded mozzarella cheese**
- **¼ cup shredded Parmesan cheese**
- **2 ½ Tbsp. cream cheese, cubed**
- **½ tsp. sea salt**
- **Freshly ground black pepper, to taste**
- **Coconut oil cooking spray, as needed**

How to Prepare:

Set the oven to 400 degrees F to preheat.

Fill a small pot with water and add half the sea salt. Stir, cover, and place over high flame. Bring to a boil. Once boiling, add the cauliflower florets and boil for 2 minutes or until fork tender.

Drain the cauliflower florets thoroughly and place in a colander. Set aside to drain.

Meanwhile, pour the heavy cream into a saucepan. Place over medium flame and heat through, stirring frequently. Continue to stir until the heavy cream is simmering.

Stir the Cheddar and mozzarella cheeses into the saucepan, followed by the garlic. Continue to stir until melted.

Turn off the heat and set aside. Transfer the cauliflower florets into a bowl and pour the cheese mixture on top of the cauliflower. Add the remaining salt and then season with black pepper. Toss well to coat.

Lightly coat a baking dish with coconut oil cooking spray. Spread the cauliflower and cheese mixture in the baking dish and bake for 10 minutes, or until bubbly and golden brown.

Transfer to a cooling rack and let stand for 5 minutes before serving. Best served warm.

Nutritional Information per Serving

Calories: 198

Fat: 16.8 g

Protein: 9.6 g

Carbohydrates: 2.4 g

Fiber: 0.9 g

BRAISED STUFFED PORK CHOPS IN MUSHROOM SAUCE

The braising cooking process is when you cook the meat slowly in fat within a closed pot in minimal moisture. This concentrates all the flavors from the different herbs and oils into the meat. The result is a tender masterpiece of a dish. Pack this for lunch with a side of steamed greens, broccoli, or beans. You will thank yourself later during the day.

Number of Servings: 4

You will Need:

- 4 organic, pasture-raised pork chops, 1 inch thick each
- 8 prosciutto slices, trimmed and chopped
- 2 garlic cloves, peeled and minced
- 1 cup mushrooms, such as porcini, trimmed and sliced
- 1 cup chicken bone broth
- ½ cup dry white wine
- 2 Tbsp. freshly grated Parmesan cheese
- 1 Tbsp. olive oil, plus more if needed
- 2 tsp. chopped fresh thyme
- 2 tsp. chopped fresh rosemary
- 2 tsp. almond flour
- Sea salt, to taste
- Freshly ground black pepper, to taste

How to Prepare:

Rinse the pork chops thoroughly then blot dry with paper towels. Create small slits along the sides of the pork chops to create pockets. Set aside.

In a bowl, mix together 1 teaspoon of olive oil with a pinch of salt and pepper. Stir in the dried rosemary and thyme followed by the

Parmesan cheese. Add the chopped prosciutto and mix well.

Stuff the prosciutto and cheese mixture into the pockets of the pork chops. Crimp the edges closed or secure with toothpicks, if needed. Set aside.

Place a heavy duty frying pan over medium flame and heat about a teaspoon of olive oil. Swirl to coat then stir in the garlic. Sauté until fragrant.

Stir the mushrooms into the frying pan then cover and simmer for 5 minutes, or until the mushrooms are tender. Sprinkle in the almond flour and stir well to combine.

Pour the chicken bone broth and dry white wine into the frying pan and increase to high flame. Bring to a boil.

Once boiling, reduce to low flame and simmer until slightly thickened. Season the mushroom sauce to taste with salt and pepper, then cover and set aside.

Place another large frying pan over medium high flame and heat the remaining olive oil. Add the pork chops and cook for 2 minutes per side, or until golden brown and cooked through.

Pour the mushroom sauce over the cooked stuffed pork chops, then cover and reduce to low flame. Cook for about 20 minutes or until the pork chops are tender.

Transfer the pork chops to a serving dish and spoon the mushroom sauce on top. Serve right away.

Nutritional Information per Serving

Calories: 300
Fat: 16 g
Protein: 34 g
Carbohydrates: 6 g
Fiber: 1 g

GRILLED SEAFOOD AND AVOCADO SALAD

This light salad is a satisfying lunch for any Keto dieter due to its combination of the creamy taste of avocado, the hearty succulence of tomato and bell pepper, and the zesty smoky flavor of the grilled shrimp. You can serve them right away or you can pack them for lunch at work. No need to reheat!

Number of Servings: 4

You will Need:

- 1 large or 2 small avocados
- 1 red bell pepper, cored, seeded, and chopped
- 1 large Roma tomato, chopped
- 1 small onion, peeled and chopped
- 1 ¼ lb. shrimp, peeled and deveined
- 2 ½ Tbsp. olive oil
- 1 ½ tsp. freshly squeezed lime juice
- ¾ tsp. garlic powder
- ¾ tsp. sea salt
- Freshly ground black pepper, to taste

How to Prepare:

Halve the avocado and discard the stone. Scoop out the flesh and slice into bite-sized cubes. Place in a bowl and sprinkle in the lime juice. Mix well to coat.

Add the bell pepper, tomato, and onion to the avocado mixture. Season with half the salt and toss again to combine. Cover the bowl and refrigerate until ready to serve.

Preheat the grill to medium high flame.

Meanwhile, mix together the olive oil, garlic powder, half the salt, and a pinch of black pepper. Mix well and then add the shrimp and toss well to coat.

Grill the shrimp for 2 minutes per side, or until pink, opaque, and cooked through. Transfer to a plate and set aside.

To serve, divide the salad among four plates and then add the shrimp. Serve right away, or store immediately into airtight containers and refrigerate for up to 2 days.

Nutritional Information per Serving

Calories: 409

Fat: 25 g

Protein: 36 g

Carbohydrates: 10 g

Fiber: 5.1 g

ASIAN CHICKEN SALAD

Packed with healthy fats and protein, this chicken salad will make your lunch break more special than it usually is. The spicy peanut dressing can be stored separately in an airtight container and stored in the refrigerator. You can add as much of it into your salad as you like.

Number of Servings: 4

You will Need:

- 4 organic, pasture-raised chicken breasts, skins removed
- 6 cups shredded Napa cabbage
- 2 cups shredded red cabbage
- ½ cup julienned red bell peppers
- ½ cup julienned carrot
- 2 Tbsp. chopped green onions
- 4 Tbsp. chopped fresh cilantro
- Sea salt, as needed

For the Spicy Peanut Dressing:

- 6 Tbsp. natural unsweetened peanut butter
- 6 Tbsp. peanut oil
- 4 Tbsp. rice wine vinegar
- 2 Tbsp. soy sauce
- ½ tsp cayenne pepper

How to Prepare:

First make the dressing by combining the peanut butter, peanut oil, rice wine vinegar, and soy sauce in a bowl. Whisk well until smooth. Add the cayenne pepper and blend well to combine. Adjust seasoning, if needed. Store in the refrigerator until ready to serve.

Place the chicken breasts in a saucepan and add enough water to cover. Add a pinch of salt, then cover and place over high flame and bring to a boil. Once boiling, reduce to a simmer and cook for 10 minutes, or until the chicken breasts are cooked through.

Once cooked, drain the chicken breasts thoroughly and thinly slice across the grain. Place in a large mixing bowl and add the shredded cabbages, bell pepper, carrot, green onion, and about a cupful of the spicy peanut dressing. Toss well to coat.

Divide the salad into four servings and top with fresh cilantro to garnish. Serve right away or store in airtight containers and refrigerate for up to 3 days.

Nutritional Information per Serving

Calories: 508

Fat: 34 g

Protein: 35 g

Carbohydrates: 12 g

Fiber: 6 g

SQUASH SPAGHETTI WITH MEATBALLS

One of the dishes missed by those on any low carb diet is spaghetti, mostly because of its hearty Italian flavor and texture. This particular Keto-friendly spaghetti with meatballs recipe calls for spaghetti squash, the quintessential substitute to traditional spaghetti pasta. Once cooked, you would not be able to tell the difference. In addition, spaghetti squash is rich in dietary fiber, vitamins A and C, and calcium and potassium.

Number of Servings: 4

You will Need:

- 1 large spaghetti squash
- ½ lb. 80% lean organic, grass-fed ground beef
- ¼ lb. lean organic, pasture-raised ground pork
- 1 garlic clove, minced
- ½ cup organic, sugar-free tomato sauce
- ½ cup chopped fresh parsley
- ¼ cup shredded Parmesan cheese
- 3 Tbsp. water
- 2 Tbsp. coconut oil
- 1 Tbsp. chopped fresh oregano
- 1 Tbsp. chopped fresh basil
- ¼ tsp. onion powder
- Sea salt, to taste
- Freshly ground black pepper, to taste

How to Prepare:

Combine the ground beef and pork into a bowl and add the basil, oregano, garlic, onion powder, salt, pepper, and 2 tablespoons of Parmesan cheese. Mix well with clean hands then cover the bowl with plastic wrap and refrigerate.

Halve the spaghetti squash lengthwise. Scoop out and discard the seeds. Place the spaghetti squash in a microwaveable glass dish and add the water. Microwave for 12 minutes on high.

Carefully remove the spaghetti squash from the microwave using pot holders. Scoop the spaghetti squash flesh from the shells using a fork and shred. Transfer into a bowl and set aside.

Place a saucepan over medium high flame and heat through. Once hot, add half a tablespoon of olive oil and swirl to coat. Stir in the spaghetti squash and sauté until golden brown and slightly dried. Place back into the bowl and fold in 2 tablespoons of the parsley. Set aside.

Take the meat out of the refrigerator. Divide into 8 equal pieces and shape into meatballs. Set aside.

Place a large frying pan over medium high flame and heat through. Once hot, add the coconut oil and swirl to coat. Cook the meatballs for 2 minutes per side or until browned all over.

Pour the tomato sauce into the pan and stir to completely cover the meatballs. Reduce to low flame and cover. Simmer for 10 minutes, or until the meatballs are completely cooked.

Divide the spaghetti squash into four servings and then divide the meatballs among them. Top with the tomato sauce and remaining Parmesan cheese. Serve warm, or refrigerate for up to 3 days for lunch on-the-go. Reheat before serving.

Nutritional Information per Serving

Calories: 460

Fat: 28 g

Protein: 43 g

Carbohydrates: 9.6 g

Fiber: 1.3 g

HERBED CREAMY CHEESE PORK CHOPS

Are you in the mood for a Keto gourmet lunch? If you are, then this is the recipe you are looking for! This dish is pork chops smothered in herbed cream cheese with a generous heap of seasoned goat cheese on top. Best served with a light green salad for added flair and flavor.

Number of Servings: 4

You will Need:

- 4 organic, pasture-raised pork chops, boneless
- 1 shallot, chopped
- 3 garlic cloves,
- 8 oz. goat cheese
- 1 cup heavy cream
- ½ cup sliced mushrooms
- 3 Tbsp. sherry
- 3 Tbsp. grass-fed butter
- 1 Tbsp. olive oil
- 1 Tbsp. and 1 tsp. chopped fresh oregano
- 1 Tbsp. and 1 tsp. chopped fresh thyme
- 1 Tbsp. finely chopped fresh rosemary
- Sea salt, to taste
- Freshly ground black pepper, to taste

How to Prepare:

Peel the garlic cloves. Roughly chop two garlic cloves and minced one. Set aside.

Rinse the pork chops and then blot dry with paper towels. Season both sides with salt and pepper and set aside.

Place a frying pan over medium flame and heat through. Once hot, cook each pork chop for 4 minutes per side and place on a platter lined with paper towels. Set aside.

Wipe the frying pan clean and place over medium flame. Add the butter and swirl to coat. Sauté the shallot and the roughly chopped garlic until fragrant. Then, stir in the mushrooms and sauté until tender.

Stir in the sherry and 1 tablespoon each of the rosemary, thyme, and oregano. Scrape the bottom of the frying pan to loosen the browned bits of pork. Stir them into the mixture. Increase to high flame and bring to a boil.

Once boiling, reduce to medium flame and simmer until the sherry is reduced by half. Then, add the heavy cream and stir to combine.

Return the cooked pork chops back into the frying pan and turn several times in the creamy sauce to coat. Cover the frying pan and simmer for 5 minutes, or until the pork chops are tender.

Meanwhile, combine the goat cheese with the minced garlic and the 1 teaspoon each of thyme and oregano. Mix well.

Divide the goat cheese mixture among the pork chops and cover. Cook for 1 minute or until the cheese is melted.

Transfer the pork chops and sauce onto serving plates and serve right away, or store in airtight containers and refrigerate for up to 3 days. Reheat before serving.

Nutritional Information per Serving

Calories: 751

Fat: 60 g

Protein: 42 g

Carbohydrates: 5 g

Fiber: 1 g

ASIAN-INSPIRED TUNA WITH CAULIFLOWER RICE

Description

Number of Servings: 4

You will Need:

- **4 tuna fillets, 8 oz. each**
- **2 ½ cups chopped cauliflower florets**
- **2 Tbsp. minced fresh ginger**
- **2 tsp. olive oil**
- **2 tsp. soy sauce or tamari sauce**
- **1 tsp. sesame oil**
- **1 tsp. rice wine vinegar**

How to Prepare:

Set the oven to 400 degrees F to preheat. Line a baking dish with aluminum foil and set aside.

Combine the sesame and olive oils with the rice wine vinegar and soy sauce or tamari sauce. Add the minced fresh ginger and mix well.

Rinse the tuna fillets and blot dry with paper towels. Place in the baking dish and pour the mixture on top. Turn twice to coat.

Bake for 15 to 20 minutes, or until the tuna fillets have an internal temperature of at least 125 degrees F.

While the tuna fillets are cooking, place the cauliflower florets into a food processor and shred into rice-like grains. Spread onto a baking sheet and place in the upper rack of the oven. Bake for 5 minutes.

Once the tuna fillets are cooked and the cauliflower rice is heated through, divide the cauliflower into four servings and serve with tuna fillets. Serve right away, or store immediately into airtight containers and refrigerate for up to 3 days. Reheat before serving.

Nutritional Information per Serving

Calories: 539

Fat: 39 g

Protein: 41.8 g

Carbohydrates: 5 g

Fiber: 2.3 g

CLASSIC PORK STEW

This savory pork stew is extremely low in carb and rich in fat and protein. To add more fat, stir in a dollop of heavy cream. Serve piping hot with roasted cauliflower or broccoli smothered in cream cheese for lunch or even dinner.

Number of Servings: 4

You will Need:

- 1 ½ lb. boneless organic, pasture-raised pork loin
- 2 ¾ cups chicken broth
- 6 oz. sliced mushrooms
- 1 onion, peeled and quartered
- 3 garlic cloves, peeled and crushed
- ¾ cup sliced carrot
- ¾ Tbsp. olive oil
- ¾ Tbsp. butter
- ¾ tsp. sea salt
- Ground cloves, to taste
- Freshly ground black pepper

How to Prepare:

Rinse the pork loin and then blot dry with paper towels. Slice into bite-sized cubes and set aside.

Place a Dutch oven over medium flame and heat through. Once hot, add the olive oil and butter. Stir to mix then stir in the onion. Sauté until translucent.

Add the garlic and sauté until fragrant. Add the cubed pork loin and cook, stirring occasionally, until browned and tender. Stir in the carrot, mushrooms, chicken broth, salt, and a pinch of cloves and black pepper. Mix everything well.

Increase to high flame and bring to a boil. Once boiling, reduce to medium low flame, cover, and simmer for 30 to 45 minutes, or until the pork is extra tender.

Adjust seasoning if needed. Divide into individual servings and serve piping hot, or store in an airtight container and refrigerate for up to 3 days. Reheat before serving.

Nutritional Information per Serving

Calories: 344

Fat: 13 g

Protein: 49 g

Carbohydrates: 5.51 g

Fiber: 1 g

VEGGIE BEEF LASAGNA

Who says you need pasta to make cheesy, beefy lasagna? This lasagna recipe calls for the use of zucchini as a replacement. Since this vegetable it only contains about 17 calories per 100 grams, it is the ultimate noodle pasta replacement for Keto dieters everywhere. Best to bake this dish ahead of time so that you can slice them into individual servings and store them in the refrigerator for quick lunch on-the-go. Reheat before serving and serve with a light salad.

Number of Servings: 4

You will Need:

- 1 large zucchini
- 1 yellow onion, peeled and chopped
- 2 garlic cloves, peeled and minced
- ½ lb. 75% lean organic, grass-fed ground beef
- 1 cup organic, sugar-free tomato sauce
- ½ cup ricotta cheese
- ¼ cup shredded Parmesan cheese
- 4 Tbsp. shredded mozzarella cheese
- 1 Tbsp. olive oil
- 1 Tbsp. chopped fresh oregano
- ½ Tbsp. chopped fresh basil
- Sea salt, to taste
- Freshly ground black pepper, to taste

How to Prepare:

Rinse the zucchini thoroughly and then slice lengthwise into 12 thin pieces. Set aside.

Set the oven to 375 degrees F to preheat.

Place a saucepan over medium high flame and heat through. Once hot, add the olive oil and swirl to coat. Sauté the onion until translucent. Add the garlic and sauté until fragrant.

Add the ground beef and sauté until browned, cooked through, and broken into tiny bits. Pour in the tomato sauce and stir. Bring to a simmer.

Once simmering, reduce to low flame and stir in the oregano, basil, and a pinch of salt to taste. Mix everything well.

In a small baking dish, create a single layer of zucchini slices using six pieces. Spoon half of the beefy tomato sauce on top, then add 2 tablespoons of ricotta cheese followed by a tablespoon of mozzarella cheese.

Repeat the layers, with the top layer being the cheeses.

Once everything has been layered, sprinkle the Parmesan cheese on top and add some more black pepper.

Bake the veggie beef lasagna for 20 to 25 minutes, or until bubbly and golden brown.

Carefully remove the lasagna from the oven and set on a cooling rack for 15 minutes. Slice into four equal portions and serve, or store in airtight containers and refrigerate for up to 3 days. Reheat before serving.

Nutritional Information per Serving

Calories: 345

Fat: 20.9 g

Protein: 24.7 g

Carbohydrates: 6 g

Fiber: 3 g

CHAPTER 6: KETO SNACK RECIPES

We are all human, so it is only natural for us to crave for something to eat in between regular meal hours. Good news is that the Keto diet not only allows but actually encourages you to enjoy small snacks after breakfast and before dinner. That way, you can avoid getting unhealthy cravings for high carb foods. Make these snacks at home and then pack them in tiny containers for when you are on the go. You should also keep them in stock in the pantry or fridge so you can always have something to nibble on before the next meal.

CHEESY FRIED AVOCADO STICKS

This tasty fried sticks have a crispy and cheesy coating, but when you sink your teeth in a little deeper, you will get to the creamy and velvetiness of the avocado. Without a doubt, they are a healthier and more flavorful alternative to any plate of sad soggy, high carb potato fries.

Number of Servings: 4

You will Need:

- 1 large organic egg
- 1 large avocado
- ¼ cup shredded Parmesan cheese
- ¼ cup ground organic pork rinds
- 1 ¼ Tbsp. heavy cream
- ¼ tsp garlic powder
- ¼ tsp onion powder
- Sea salt, to taste
- Freshly ground black pepper, to taste
- Peanut, canola, or sunflower oil, as needed

How to Prepare:

Break open the egg into a small bowl and add the heavy cream. Whisk well until creamy and smooth. Set aside.

On a plate, combine the pork rinds with the Parmesan cheese and onion and garlic powders. Set aside.

Slice the avocado in half and discard the stone. Carefully scoop out the avocado flesh, taking care not to mash anything. Slice the avocado into thick, curved sticks. Season lightly with salt and pepper.

Coat each avocado stick in the egg and heavy cream mixture. Then, dredge in the cheesy pork rind mixture. Tap excess off and set aside on a plate. Repeat with the remaining slices. Set aside.

Place a deep frying pan over low flame and add about 1.5 inches of cooking oil. Heat the oil to 375 degrees F.

Once the oil is ready, carefully place each avocado stick into it. Do not overcrowd. Deep fry for approximately 1 minute and 30 seconds and then immediately remove with a slotted spoon and place on a plate lined with paper towels.

Let the avocado sticks stand for about 5 minutes to become extra crispy. Best served warm, but not piping hot.

Nutritional Information per Serving

Calories: 346

Fat: 27 g

Protein: 21 g

Carbohydrates: 3 g

Fiber: 4 g

CHEESY CAULIFLOWER BITES

Popcorn is tasty, but it is also high in carbs. Luckily, these Cheesy Cauliflower Bites are more than just an alternative because they taste better. Each mouthful is bursting with herbed mozzarella goodness, you will forget you are eating a cruciferous vegetable as a snack!

Number of Servings: 4

You will Need:

- 1 large organic egg
- 1 cup finely chopped cauliflower florets
- 2 Tbsp. roughly chopped organic pork rinds
- ½ cup fresh mozzarella
- ¼ cup almond flour
- 1 tsp. dried tarragon or basil

How to Prepare:

Preheat the oven to 110 degrees F to preheat. Line a baking sheet with parchment paper and set aside.

Combine the chopped organic pork rinds, almond flour, and dried tarragon or basil in a bowl. Mix well and set aside.

In a separate bowl, whisk the egg and add the cauliflower florets. Mix well until evenly coated.

Combine the cauliflower mixture with the flour mixture until all the ingredients are evenly distributed. Divide the mixture into bite-sized balls.

Arrange the balls on the prepared baking sheet and bake for 5 minutes, or until golden brown.

Transfer to a cooling rack and let stand for 5 minutes. Best served warm. Store any leftovers in an airtight container and refrigerate for up to 3 days.

Nutritional Information per Serving

Calories: 85

Fat: 15 g

Protein: 8 g

Carbohydrates: 1 g

Fiber: 0.4 g

BARBEQUE TOFU FRIES

Looking for a crispy, hearty snack or a savory, spiced side dish to your favorite Keto patties and meatballs? Try these barbeque tofu fries right away! You can also munch on these with unsweetened tomato ketchup or with a cheesy dip as a chilly afternoon snack.

Number of Servings: 4

You will Need:

- **24 oz. extra for, tofu**
- **2 Tbsp. sea salt**
- **4 tsp. freshly ground black pepper**
- **2 tsp. garlic powder**
- **2 tsp. ground cumin**
- **2 tsp. dried parsley**
- **1 tsp. onion powder**
- **½ tsp. paprika**
- **½ tsp. cayenne pepper**
- **Coconut, peanut or sunflower oil, as needed**

How to Prepare:

Pour about 3 inches of cooking oil in a heavy duty pot and place over medium flame. Heat to about 350 degrees F.

Drain the tofu thoroughly and then slice into quarter-inch pieces. Pat dry with paper towels and place on paper towels to drain.

On a plate, combine the parsley, garlic powder, onion powder, paprika, cayenne pepper, cumin, salt, and black pepper. Mix well.

Coat the tofu fries thoroughly in the mixture and then set aside.

Cook the tofu fries in the oil for about 2 minutes per side, or until golden brown and crisp. Cook in batches, if needed. Once cooked, immediately transfer the tofu fries to a plate lined with paper towels and allow to drain completely, about 3 minutes.

Serve the tofu fries warm or at room temperature with a dip on the side, if desired.

Nutritional Information per Serving

Calories: 197

Fat: 14.3 g

Protein: 14 g

Carbohydrates: 6.5 g

Fiber: 2.5 g

CAJUN TRAIL MIX

On chilly movie nights, you will definitely want to whip out a container full of these tasty and slightly spicy mixed nuts. The blend of spices and dried herbs give this recipe a distinctively Cajun flavor, and that is what makes this such nice treat for the grownups and the adventurous kiddies, too.

Number of Servings: 4 (1 / 3 cup per serving)

You will Need:

- ½ cup pecans
- ½ cup dry roasted peanuts
- ½ cup chopped raw cashews
- 2 Tbsp. melted grass-fed butter
- ½ tsp. paprika
- ½ tsp. Worcestershire sauce
- ¼ tsp. onion powder
- ¼ tsp. garlic powder
- Cayenne pepper, to taste
- Dried oregano, to taste
- Dried thyme, to taste
- Fine sea salt, tot aste
- Freshly ground black pepper, to taste

How to Prepare:

Set the oven to 300 degrees F to preheat.

Mix the nuts well in a baking pan and then spread out into an even layer. Set aside.

Combine the melted butter the Worcestershire sauce. Add the paprika, onion and garlic powders, and a pinch each of cayenne pepper, and dried oregano and thyme.

Mix everything well and then pour it over the nuts. Stir to coat and then spread out again into an even layer.

Roast the nuts for 25 minutes, stirring once every 10 minutes.

Once roasted, transfer to a cooling rack and let stand for about 5 minutes. After that, season to taste with salt and transfer to an airtight container. Store in a cool, dry shelf for up to 3 weeks.

Nutritional Information per Serving

Calories: 306

Fat: 28 g

Protein: 7 g

Carbohydrates: 10 g

Fiber: 3 g

CHEESY ARTICHOKE AND SPINACH SPREAD

Artichokes and spinach are rich in antioxidants and fiber, so it will do you a lot of good to sneak them into your meals every chance you get. This cheesy spread is one perfect suggestion, especially since it is so tasty and goes so well with sliced cucumber, parsnip, celery, and jicama sticks.

Number of Servings: 4

You will Need:

- 1 cup artichoke hearts, chopped
- ¾ cup spinach, chopped
- ½ cup Parmesan cheese
- ¼ cup shredded mozzarella cheese
- ¼ cup shredded Gruyere cheese
- 4 oz. cream cheese
- 1 garlic clove, peeled and minced
- 1 Tbsp. grass-fed butter
- 1 ½ Tbsp. sour cream
- ¼ tsp. paprika
- ¼ tsp. sea salt
- ¼ tsp. freshly ground black pepper

How to Prepare:

Set the oven to 375 degrees F to preheat.

Place a frying pan over medium high flame and heat through. Once hot, add the butter and swirl to coat. Sauté the minced garlic until fragrant.

Stir the spinach into the garlic butter and sauté until wilted. Stir in the artichoke hearts and sauté until heated through. Transfer the mixture into a bowl and set aside.

Meanwhile, reduce the heat to low flame and stir in the cream cheese. Stir until melted and smooth. Add half the Parmesan cheese and all of the mozzarella and Gruyere cheeses. Stir well until melted.

Pour the melted cheeses into the bowl of spinach and artichoke. Mix well until completely combined. Add the sour cream, paprika, salt, and pepper. Mix well.

Transfer the mixture into a large ramekin and spread into an even layer. Top with the remaining Parmesan cheese.

Bake the spread for 10 to 12 minutes, or until bubbly and golden brown.

Transfer the spread on a cooling rack and let stand for about 5 minutes. Serve warm or cool.

Nutritional Information per Serving

Calories: 259

Fat: 20.3 g

Protein: 12.5 g

Carbohydrates: 5.8 g

Fiber: 3.6 g

SAVORY SPINACH STUFFED MUSHROOMS

These hearty snacks are fun to make and even more fun to eat. Portobello mushroom is a popular Keto recipe because it is super low in calories but has that satisfying flavor and texture that adds bulk to any meal. The spinach gives this snack a lot of healthy nutrients and fiber as well. Of course, since it has cream cheese and Parmesan cheese, even the pickiest of eaters would not hesitate to indulge

Number of Servings: 4

You will Need:

- 10 oz. frozen chopped spinach, thawed
- 1 lb. Portobello mushrooms
- 6 garlic cloves, peeled and chopped
- 4 oz. cream cheese
- ½ cup chopped onion
- ¼ cup Parmesan cheese
- 2 Tbsp. grass-fed butter
- 1 ½ tsp. Worcestershire sauce
- ½ tsp. sea salt
- ¼ tsp. freshly ground black pepper

How to Prepare:

Set the oven to 350 degrees F to preheat.

Rinse the Portobello mushrooms thoroughly then slice off the stems. Mince the stems and place in a bowl and set aside.

Place the spinach in a colander to thaw completely.

Place a large frying pan over medium low flame and heat through. Once hot, stir in the butter until melted. Stir in the onion and minced mushrooms stems and sauté until tender. Stir in the garlic and sauté until fragrant.

Once the spinach is thawed, press out all excess liquids before stirring into the frying pan with the mushroom mixture. Stir until wilted.

Add the cream cheese, salt, pepper, Worcestershire sauce, and Parmesan cheese into the spinach mixture. Mix well.

Divide the spinach mixture among the mushroom caps. Arrange the stuffed mushrooms in a baking dish.

Pour just enough water around the mushroom caps, taking care not to let water get into the caps. Then, bake for 30 minutes.

Carefully remove from the oven and transfer the stuffed mushrooms to a serving platter. Best served warm.

Nutritional Information per Serving

Calories: 240

Fat: 8 g

Protein: 4 g

Carbohydrates: 4 g

Fiber: 4 g

SAVORY KALE CHIPS

Kale is rich in fiber and extremely low in calories, in that a cupful contains only 36. It is also rich in folate, magnesium, and a host of other nutrients, so snacking on it should not make you feel guilty at all. So, go ahead and toss those nasty processed potato chips into the bin and replace them with a bowlful of these crispy, savory kale chips!

Number of Servings: 4

You will Need:

- **4 cups kale leaves**
- **2 Tbsp. olive oil**
- **1 tsp. garlic powder**
- **1 tsp. onion powder**
- **1 tsp. fine sea salt**
- **1 tsp. freshly ground black pepper**

How to Prepare:

Set the oven to 300 degrees F to preheat. Line two baking sheets with parchment paper and set aside.

Spread each kale leaf out and then massage both sides with olive oil. Sprinkle both sides with the onion and garlic powders, followed by the salt and pepper.

Lay the seasoned kale leaves in a single layer on the prepared baking sheets. Place one baking sheet in the upper rack and the other in the middle rack.

Bake for 10 minutes, then turn the baking sheets around and switch their places on the racks. Bake for an additional 10 to 15 minutes, taking care not to burn the kale leaves.

Carefully remove the baking sheets from the oven and place on a cooling rack. Allow to cool for about 5 minutes and then serve. Store extra servings in an airtight container at room temperature, away from direct sunlight.

Nutritional Information per Serving

Calories: 99

Fat: 7 g

Protein: 2.2 g

Carbohydrates: 7.2 g

Fiber: 1.2 g

SOUTHWESTERN STUFFED EGGS

Spicy stuffed eggs are definitely a crowd pleaser! You can whip up this batch for your family and friends as a nice snack or appetizer before a big meal. The yogurt and mayonnaise give it a smooth and creamy filling, with the minced onion, vinegar, garlic, and chili powder packing in a punch.

Number of Servings: 4 (4 pieces per serving)

You will Need:

- 8 large, organic eggs
- 3 Tbsp. mayonnaise
- 1 ½ Tbsp. low fat yogurt
- 1 ½ Tbsp. minced onion
- 1 ½ Tbsp. cider vinegar
- 1 tsp. chili powder
- ¼ tsp. minced garlic
- Sea salt, as needed

How to Prepare:

Place the eggs in a pot and fill it with water. Add a pinch of salt. Cover and place over high flame. Bring to a boil. Once boiling reduce to a simmer and simmer for 10 minutes.

After 10 minutes, remove from heat and set aside as you prepare a bowl of ice water. When ready, transfer the eggs into the bowl of ice water and let stand for 10 minutes to cool.

Once cooled, carefully peel the eggs. Slice the eggs in half and scoop out the yolks into a bowl.

Add the mayonnaise and yogurt into the yolks and mix well. Add the minced onion, chili powder, cider vinegar, and garlic. Mix everything until smooth.

Arrange the egg whites, sliced side facing up, on a platter. Heap the mixture into the hollows and then serve right away.

Nutritional Information per Serving

Calories: 228

Fat: 20 g

Protein: 12 g

Carbohydrates: 4 g

Fiber: 1 g

COCONUT BERRY SHAKE

Berries are low in sugar, high in antioxidants, and bursting with flavor. Blend them up with some smooth and creamy coconut milk and you are in for a healthy, tasty, and super filling snack on the go. For best results, freeze the berries and chill the coconut milk before blending them up.

Number of Servings: 1

You will Need:

- ½ cup crushed ice
- ¼ cup pure coconut milk
- ¼ cup frozen blackberries
- ¼ cup frozen raspberries
- ¼ cup frozen blueberries
- ½ Tbsp. cold-pressed coconut oil
- ¼ tsp. pure vanilla extract

How to Prepare:

Pour half the crushed ice into a high speed blender and add the coconut oil and coconut milk. Cover and blend until smooth.

Pour in the frozen berries and the remaining crushed ice. Blend for about a minute or until smooth and creamy.

Pour into a tall glass and serve right away.

Nutritional Information per Serving

Calories: 252
Fat: 21.6 g
Protein: 2.5 g
Carbohydrates: 9.7 g
Fiber: 6.1 g

SPICY GUACAMOLE WITH BACON BITS

Are you looking for a spicy dip for your celery and cucumber sticks? Especially one particular dip with a Mexican flare? If so, then look no further than this special guacamole recipe because it will surely satisfy your cravings! Topped with crispy bacon bits, it will make your snack-time something to look forward to each day! Of course, you can always make it non-spicy if you are not into that by simply removing the jalapeno pepper. Really, do whatever floats your boat!

Number of Servings: 3

You will Need:

- 3 organic bacon strips
- 1 large avocado
- 1 tomato, any kind, chopped
- ½ yellow onion, peeled and chopped
- 1 small garlic clove, minced
- 1 jalapeno pepper, seeded (if desired) and minced
- ½ Tbsp. chopped fresh cilantro
- ½ tsp. freshly squeezed lime juice
- Sea salt, to taste
- Freshly ground black pepper, to taste

How to Prepare:

Place a large frying pan over medium high flame and heat through. Once hot, add the bacon strips and cook for 3 minutes per side, or until crisp. Transfer to a plate lined with paper towels and set aside.

Meanwhile, halve the avocado and discard the stone. Scoop the avocado flesh out of the skins and place them in a bowl. Add the chopped tomato and onion and then mix in the freshly squeezed lime juice. Add the garlic and jalapeno pepper, mixing in until well combined.

Chop the cooled bacon and fold into the guacamole. Season to taste with salt and pepper, taking care not to over-mix it into a mush. Best served right away.

Nutritional Information per Serving

Calories: 259

Fat: 22.8 g

Protein: 5.1 g

Carbohydrates: 4.1 g

Fiber: 7.5 g

CHAPTER 7: KETO DINNER RECIPES

The quintessential Keto-friendly dinner is a bowlful of hot meat stew with a side of steamed greens and other low carb veggies during chilly nights. If the weather is warm, a nice light green salad with an accompaniment of roasted or baked meat and a dollop of sour cream should do the trick. The best part is that you can make them all within the comforts of your home using easy-to-find ingredients. This chapter will show you some of the best Keto dinner recipes to start with.

BEEF STROGANOFF

This hearty beef dish has been a favorite on the dinner table since it was first conceptualized in mid-19th century Russia. And it is no wonder, for despite its simple and easy to find ingredients, Beef Stroganoff never fails to satisfy your taste buds. With this Keto version, you can even double up the recipe so that you can store leftovers in the freezer for easy reheating in the week ahead.

Number of Servings: 4

You will Need:

- 1 lb. organic, grass-fed beef roast
- 2 garlic cloves, peeled and minced
- 1 large yellow onion, peeled and minced
- 4 cups chopped green cabbage
- 1 ½ cups organic beef bone broth
- 1 cup chopped mushrooms
- ½ cup cream cheese, at room temperature
- ½ cup heavy cream
- 1 Tbsp. olive oil
- 1 tsp. tomato paste
- Sea salt, to taste
- Freshly ground black pepper, to taste

How to Prepare:

In a bowl, combine the beef bone broth, cream cheese, heavy cream, and tomato paste. Mix well and set aside.

Rinse the beef roast thoroughly and then blot dry with paper towels. Season all over with salt and pepper and then set aside.

Place a Dutch oven over medium high flame and heat through. Once hot, add the olive oil and swirl to coat. Add the beef roast and cook until browned all over. Transfer the beef roast to a platter and set aside.

Stir the onion and mushrooms into the Dutch oven and sauté until tender. Add the garlic and sauté until the garlic is fragrant. Transfer everything into a bowl and set aside.

Spread the chopped green cabbage in the bottom of the Dutch oven. Add the beef roast on top, followed by the onion and mushrooms mixture.

Pour the cream cheese and tomato paste mixture over the beef, then cover and cook over low flame for 3 hours, or until the beef roast is extra tender.

Carefully remove from the heat and uncover. Shred the beef roast and serve. Best served warm with the cabbage.

Nutritional Information per Serving

Calories: 438

Fat: 26.9 g

Protein: 40 g

Carbohydrates: 5.8 g

Fiber: 2.3 g

CHEESY CHICKEN THIGHS STUFFED WITH KALE AND BACON

Imagine coming home after a hard day's work to a hot and delicious dinner of savory chicken thighs stuffed with finely chopped kale, cream and Swiss cheeses, butter, garlic, and bacon. For added fiber and nutrients, it is best to serve this delightful dish with a light salad.

Number of Servings: 4

You will Need:

- 1 lb. organic, pasture-raised boneless chicken thighs
- 5 organic bacon strips
- 2 garlic cloves, peeled and minced
- 1 ½ cups finely chopped kale leaves
- ¾ cup cream cheese, at room temperature
- ¼ cup shredded Swiss cheese
- 2 Tbsp. grass-fed butter
- ¼ tsp. sea salt
- ¼ tsp. freshly ground black pepper

How to Prepare:

Set the oven to 425 degrees F to preheat.

Lay the bacon strips on a baking sheet and bake for 12 to 15 minutes, or until crisp and browned. Remove from the oven and set aside.

Place a large frying pan over medium high flame and heat through. Add the butter and swirl to coat. Stir in the garlic and kale leaves and sauté until the kale leaves start to wilt. Transfer the mixture into a bowl.

Chop the bacon into small bits and add to the kale leaves. Fold in the cream cheese until melted and completely combined. Set aside.

Place the chicken thighs on a clean flat surface and spread out wide. Divide the kale and bacon mixture among the chicken thighs, then fold them over. Secure with toothpicks and arrange on a baking dish.

Season the chicken thighs with salt and pepper. Then, divide the Swiss cheese among them. Bake for 20 minutes, or until the internal temperature of the chicken thighs reach 165 degrees F per serving.

Once cooked, transfer the baking sheet on a cooling rack and let stand for 5 minutes. Best served warm.

Nutritional Information per Serving

Calories: 527

Fat: 44 g

Protein: 29 g

Carbohydrates: 2.4 g

Fiber: 0 g

PROVENCAL BEEF STEW

Stews might seem bothersome to make, but the truth is they are quite easy because all you have to do is throw everything into the pot and cook over low flame! So go ahead and try this classic French beef stew. It is best cooked and served during a chilly weekend, but the dish also refrigerates splendidly for easy reheating later during the week. Serve this with steamed cauliflower or zucchini noodles for added flavor, fiber, and nutrients.

Number of Servings: 4

You will Need:

- 2 lb. stewing beef, sliced into large cubes
- 2 medium red onions, peeled and chopped
- 2 medium carrots, peeled and sliced into thin rounds
- 1 celery stalk, trimmed and chopped
- 1 fennel bulb, trimmed and chopped
- 3 garlic cloves, peeled and crushed
- 2 bay leaves
- 1 ½ inches orange zest strips
- 1 ½ cups beef bone broth
- ¾ cup dry red wine
- ½ cup chopped fresh flat leaf parsley
- ¾ Tbsp. dried thyme
- 1/8 tsp. whole black peppercorns
- Sea salt, to taste

How to Prepare:

Two days before serving, mix together all of the ingredients in a large Dutch oven. Cover and refrigerate for 24 hours.

After 24 hours, place the Dutch oven over the lowest possible flame and heat, covered, until simmering. Continue to simmer for 2 hours, or until the stewing beef becomes extra tender.

Carefully remove the Dutch oven from the flame and set aside. Allow to cool to room temperature, then skim off the solidified fat that rises to the surface with a spoon.

Reheat the stew over medium flame and let simmer for 10 minutes. Season to taste with salt and pepper, if needed, then discard the bay leaves. Ladle into soup bowls and serve piping hot.

Nutritional Information per Serving

Calories: 374

Fat: 16 g

Protein: 46 g

Carbohydrates: 9 g

Fiber: 2 g

CHICKEN AVOCADO LETTUCE WRAPS

At first glance, these chicken avocado lettuce wraps look like one of the simplest dinners you could ever have. But take one bite and you will get a full burst of flavor and texture from the myriad of ingredients in them. Packed with protein and healthy fats, this recipe is a quintessential Keto dinner treat!

Number of Servings: 4

You will Need:

- 1 lb. organic, pasture-raised ground chicken
- 1 large avocado
- 4 large lettuce leaves
- 2 garlic cloves, peeled and minced
- ½ cup almond flour
- 2 Tbsp. olive oil
- 1 Tbsp. freshly squeezed lemon juice
- 1 tsp. onion powder
- ¼ tsp. sea salt
- Freshly ground black pepper, to taste

How to Prepare:

Slice the avocado in half and then discard the stone. Scoop out the meat and place in a bowl. Add the lemon juice and mix to coat.

Add the ground chicken into the bowl of avocado. Then, add the minced garlic, onion powder, almond flour, salt, and a generous pinch of black pepper. Mix gently with clean hands, taking care not to over-mix.

Form the mixture into four large patties and place on a platter. Set aside.

Place a large frying pan over medium flame and heat through. Once hot, add the olive oil and swirl to coat. Cook the chicken avocado patties, taking care not to overcrowd. Cook for about 8 minutes per side, or until cooked through and golden brown.

Lay the lettuce leaves on a plate and place a chicken avocado patty on top of each. Serve right away.

Nutritional Information per Serving

Calories: 413

Fat: 25.7 g

Protein: 33 g

Carbohydrates: 2.9 g

Fiber: 5 g

HERB, SCALLION, AND MUSHROOM STUFFED LAMB CHOPS

Lamb chops are rich in fat and vitamin B, and by adding some herbs, onions, and mushrooms in them they become even more nutritious. Serve this on a relaxing weekend or on nights when you are in the mood to eat at home like you are in a five-star restaurant. Best to serve it with steamed greens or a light salad.

Number of Servings: 4

You will Need:

- 4 organic lamb chops, 1 inch thick
- 4 scallions, trimmed and chopped
- 5 garlic cloves
- ½ lb. mushrooms
- 2/3 cup dry red wine
- 5 Tbsp. olive oil
- 4 Tbsp. chopped fresh flat leaf parsley.
- 2 Tbsp. freshly squeezed lemon juice
- 2 Tbsp. chopped fresh rosemary
- 1 tsp. dried thyme or oregano
- Sea salt, to taste
- Freshly ground black pepper, to taste

How to Prepare:

Rinse the lamb chops and then blot dry with paper towels. Slice along the thickest area of each lamb chop to create a "pocket." Set aside.

In a large bowl, combine the freshly squeezed lemon juice with the fresh rosemary. Mix well then stir in the dry red wine, and 4 tablespoons of olive oil.

Take three garlic cloves and crush with the handle of a knife. Peel off the skins and place the crushed garlic into the wine and olive oil mixture. Whisk well.

Place the lamb chops in the marinade. Turn several times to coat, rubbing the mixture into the pockets you had created. Cover the bowl and refrigerate for 4 to 6 hours to marinate.

Before cooking the lamb chops, turn on the grill or broiler to preheat. Place the broiling pan or rack approximately 5 inches away from the flame or heat source.

Slice off the stems from the mushrooms and store away. Clean and slice the mushroom caps, then set aside.

Place a large frying pan over medium flame and heat through. Add the remaining olive oil and swirl to coat. Sauté the scallions and garlic together until tender. Then, stir in the mushrooms and sauté for about 10 minutes. Season to taste with salt and pepper. Stir in the parsley and oregano, mixing well. Turn off the heat and set aside.

Take the lamb chops out of the refrigerator and remove them from the marinade; do not discard the marinade. Blot dry with paper towels.

Divide the mushroom and scallion mixture into four equal portions. Stuff the lamb chops with the mixture and press to seal.

Broil or grill the lamb chops, basting all throughout with the marinade. For rare, cook for 4 minutes per side; for medium rare, 7 minutes per side; for well done, 9 minutes per side.

Transfer to a platter and serve right away.

Nutritional Information per Serving

Calories: 278

Fat: 22 g

Protein: 16 g

Carbohydrates: 4 g

Fiber: 1 g

CHICKEN CHILI

Cook a batch of this Keto-friendly Chicken Chili and serve on chilly nights for instant warmth and comfort. On top of that, you will also get plenty of flavor and protein. Serve it with steamed cauliflower or broccoli for added nutrients, fiber, and satisfaction.

Number of Servings: 4

You will Need:

- ¾ lb. organic, pasture-raised ground chicken
- 1 red or yellow bell pepper, cored, seeded, and diced
- 1 turnip, peeled and cubed
- 1 red onion, peeled and chopped
- 2 garlic cloves, peeled and minced
- 5.5 oz. sour cream
- 2 oz. diced green chilies
- 1 ¾ cups organic chicken bone broth
- ¾ cup shredded Cheddar cheese
- 2 Tbsp. grass-fed butter
- ¾ tsp. cumin
- ¾ tsp. chili powder
- ¾ tsp. dried oregano
- ½ tsp. cayenne pepper
- ½ tsp. sea salt
- ½ tsp. freshly ground black pepper

How to Prepare:

Place a heavy duty pot over medium high flame and heat through. Once hot, add the butter and swirl to melt. Stir in the onion and stir for 5 minutes, or until translucent.

Stir the cubed turnip, chopped bell pepper, green chilies, and garlic into the pot. Sauté until tender. Then, add the ground chicken and sauté until crumbled and browned all over.

Pour the chicken bone broth into the pot and stir well to combine. Sprinkle in the cumin, chili powder, cayenne pepper, and oregano. Mix well, then bring to a boil. Once boiling, reduce to low flame and cover.

Cook on low flame for 20 minutes, then uncover and simmer until thickened. Season to taste with the salt and pepper.

Ladle the chili into soup bowls and top with the Cheddar cheese and a dollop of sour cream. Best served piping hot.

Nutritional Information per Serving

Calories: 413

Fat: 28 g

Protein: 30 g

Carbohydrates: 6.8 g

Fiber: 1.6 g

MEDITERRANEAN SEAFOOD, SAUSAGE AND PEPPER STEW

When it comes to combining nature's bounty into one pot, the Mediterranean locals sure are experts! This stew combines pork sausage with clams, mussels, peppers, and vegetables, and while that might sound a bit odd, it is actually really popular across the region. In fact, each country has its own twist to the recipe. Serve this stew as is, or ladle it over some hot cauliflower rice to make it an even heartier meal for dinner. You can also refrigerate any leftovers and serve another bowlful for lunch the next day.

Number of Servings: 4

You will Need:

- ¼ lb. organic pork sausage, trimmed and diced
- ½ lb. small clams (such as littleneck), scrubbed
- ½ lb. unshelled mussels, trimmed and scrubbed
- 1 large ripe tomato, peeled, seeded and chopped
- 1 small red bell pepper, cored, seeded, and diced
- 1 small fennel bulb, halved and diced
- 1 red onion, peeled and sliced thinly
- 1 garlic clove, peeled and minced
- ½ cup fish broth
- ¼ cup Kalamata olives, pitted and chopped
- ¼ cup dry white wine
- 1 ½ Tbsp. chopped fresh flat leaf parsley
- ½ Tbsp. olive oil

How to Prepare:

Place a saucepan over medium flame and heat through. Once hot, add the olive oil and swirl to coat. Stir in the onion, fennel, bell pepper, and garlic and then sauté until tender.

Stir the sausage into the saucepan and sauté until cooked through. Then, add the chopped tomato with its juices. Bring to a simmer.

Once simmering, pour in the dry white wine and stir well to combine. Increase to high flame and bring to a boil.

Once boiling, reduce to low flame and cover. Let simmer for about 6 minutes, or until the liquids are reduced by half.

Stir in the fish broth and increase to high flame. Stir in the clams and mussels, then cover and reduce to medium high flame. Cook for 10 minutes, or until the clams and mussels open up.

Remove any shells that remain unopened. After that, stir in the olives and remove from the flame. Add the parsley and stir well to combine.

Ladle the stew into soup bowls and serve piping hot.

Nutritional Information per Serving

Calories: 221

Fat: 16 g

Protein: 12 g

Carbohydrates: 8 g

Fiber: 2 g

THAI-INSPIRED BROILED CHICKEN SKEWERS

Thai food is known for its delectable blend of spicy, zesty, and herby flavors, with ginger, cilantro, and red chili paste taking center-stage. You can get a taste of that for dinner by recreating this simple recipe. Serve this with some steamed greens sprinkled with lemon juice and olive oil to make it even more satisfying.

Number of Servings: 4

You will Need:

- 1 lb. organic, pasture-raised boneless chicken breast
- 2 red bell pepper
- 1 red onion
- 2 garlic cloves, peeled and minced
- 1 cup chopped fresh cilantro
- ¼ cup red chili paste
- 2 Tbsp. soy sauce or tamari sauce
- 2 Tbsp. melted coconut oil
- 1 tsp. freshly minced ginger
- 1 tsp. onion powder
- Freshly ground black pepper

How to Prepare:

Rinse the chicken breasts thoroughly and then blot dry with paper towels. Slice the chicken breasts into 1-inch cubes and set aside.

In a non-reactive bowl, combine the melted coconut oil with red chili paste, soy sauce or tamari sauce, onion powder, ginger, garlic, cilantro, and a pinch of black pepper, or to taste. Mix well.

Add the sliced chicken meat into the bowl and toss well to coat.

Cover the bowl and transfer to the refrigerator to marinate for 20 minutes.

Set the oven to broil to preheat. Set the rack in the lowest section of the oven. Line a baking sheet with aluminum foil.

Core and seed the bell peppers then slice them into large cubes. Peel the red onion and slice into large pieces as well.

Take the marinated chicken out of the refrigerator. With metal skewers, skewer the chicken, bell peppers, and onions. Lay the skewers on the prepared baking sheet.

Broil the chicken skewers for 3 minutes. Then, turn them over and broil for an additional 3 minutes. Turn one more time and cook for 3 minutes, or until the internal temperature of the chicken reaches 165 degrees F.

Once cooked, carefully transfer the chicken skewers to a plate and serve right away.

Nutritional Information per Serving

Calories: 355

Fat: 25 g

Protein: 21.7 g

Carbohydrates: 9 g

Fiber: 2.2 g

BEEF TACO SALAD WRAPS

Who does not love Mexican flavors? Almost everyone around the world does, and if you consider yourself included in the fan club, then this recipe will become your instant favorite. Instead of corn taco shells, though, this one calls for the use of extremely low carb lettuce. To make your lettuce extra crisp, place the lettuce leaves in a bowl of ice water and soak for 30 minutes. Try it and enjoy!

Number of Servings: 4

You will Need:

- 1 iceberg lettuce, leaves separated
- 1 lb. organic, grass-fed 80% lean ground beef
- 1 large avocado
- 1 green bell pepper, cored, seeded, and diced
- 1 jalapeno pepper, seeded and diced
- 2 red onions, peeled and diced
- 6 oz. diced tomatoes
- ½ cup shredded Cheddar cheese
- ¼ cup sour cream
- 2 Tbsp. olive oil
- 2 Tbsp. chopped fresh cilantro
- 2 Tbsp. freshly squeezed lime juice
- ½ tsp. cumin
- ½ tsp. paprika
- Sea salt, to taste
- Freshly ground black pepper, to taste

How to Prepare:

Place a large frying pan over medium high flame and heat through.

Once hot, add the olive oil and swirl to coat. Add the onion and sauté until translucent. Add the garlic and sauté until fragrant.

Stir in the bell pepper, half the diced tomatoes, and the jalapeno pepper. Sauté until tender.

Stir in the ground beef and sauté for about 10 minutes, or until browned, crumbled, and cooked through.

Sprinkle the cumin and paprika over everything and mix well. Season to taste with salt and pepper. Mix well.

Transfer the beef taco mixture into a bowl. Add the remaining tomatoes. Set aside.

Halve the avocado and discard the stone. Scoop out the avocado flesh and slice into small cubes. Sprinkle the lime juice over the avocados and toss gently to coat. Set aside.

Divide the lettuce leaves into individual servings and spoon the beef taco mixture into each. Add the avocados, Cheddar cheese, sour cream, and chopped cilantro. Serve right away. Leftover beef taco mixture can be stored in an airtight container and refrigerated for up to 3 days.

Nutritional Information per Serving

Calories: 587

Fat: 44.5 g

Protein: 36.6 g

Carbohydrates: 5.8 g

Fiber: 5.1 g

OVEN-ROASTED BUTTER GARLIC HADDOCK WITH SWISS CHARD

Haddock has a soft and flaky texture with a delicate flavor, and it goes perfectly well with the classic blend of roasted garlic, lemon, butter. In this particular recipe, the addition of Swiss chard – a favorite in Mediterranean cuisine – gives this extremely low carb dish more fiber and a huge boost of vitamins K, A, and C as well as magnesium, manganese, potassium, and iron. If haddock is unavailable, you can substitute it with cod.

Number of Servings: 4

You will Need:

- 4 wild-caught haddock fillets, 8 oz. each
- 2 garlic cloves, peeled and minced
- 1 lb. Swiss chard, chopped
- ½ cup grass-fed butter
- 2 Tbsp. freshly squeezed lemon juice
- ½ tsp. sea salt
- ½ tsp. freshly ground black pepper

How to Prepare:

Set the oven to 400 degrees F to preheat. Line a baking sheet with aluminum foil.

Rinse the haddock fillets thoroughly and then blot dry with paper towels. Arrange the haddock fillets on the prepared baking sheet and tuck the chopped Swiss chard around them.

Sprinkle the freshly squeezed lemon juice over the haddock fillets and Swiss chard. Then, divide the butter among the haddock fillets and top everything with the minced garlic. Sprinkle the salt and pepper on top.

Cut out another sheet of aluminum foil and cover the entire baking sheet. Crimp the edges to seal and then bake for 15 to 20 minutes, based on how thick the haddock fillets are.

Carefully remove the baking sheet out of the oven and place on a cooling rack. Remove the sheet of aluminum foil and serve right away.

Nutritional Information per Serving

Calories: 317

Fat: 23.8 g

Protein: 22 g

Carbohydrates: 4 g

Fiber: 1.3 g

CHAPTER 8: KETO DESSERT RECIPES

Sugar is banned in the Keto diet, but that does not mean you could no longer enjoy the occasional dessert. With the help of these recipes, you can recreate rich and creamy Ket-approved desserts such as ice creams and cookies at home to continue to maintain your keto-adapted self.

CREAMY CHOCO COCONUT CREAM

It is too easy to miss ice cream when you are on the Keto diet, but if you cannot help yourself, then all you have to do is recreate this recipe. Within an hour or two, you can enjoy a heaping bowl full of creamy, cold, chocolate and coconut flavored cream to satisfy those cravings.

Number of Servings: 2

You will Need:

- **1 cup pure coconut milk**
- **2 Tbsp. unsweetened cocoa powder**
- **2 Tbsp. heavy cream**

How to Prepare:

In a large bowl, mix together the coconut milk, cocoa powder, and heavy cream. Whisk well, preferably with an electric mixer, until thickened and slightly stiff.

With a spatula, smooth the cream mixture into a freezer bowl. Cover and freeze for 1 to 2 hours, or until frozen but still creamy.

Divide into two servings and serve right away.

Nutritional Information per Serving

Calories: 340

Fat: 34.9 g

Protein: 4 g

Carbohydrates: 5.6 g

Fiber: 4.4 g

STRAWBERRY COCONUT CREAM POPS

Popsicles are a favorite children's snack, especially during hot and lazy summer afternoons. The conventional ones, however, are extremely high in sugar so they have to be crossed out of the list when you are on the Keto diet. However, that does not meant you should no longer enjoy a nice ice cold and creamy pop every now and then. This particular recipe will show you how to make a batch that is low in carbs but high in fat with an explosion of delicious coconut and strawberry flavors.

Number of Servings: 4

You will Need:

- 1 ½ cups chilled coconut milk
- 1 cup sliced strawberries
- ¾ cup heavy cream
- ¼ tsp. stevia

How to Prepare:

Pour the coconut milk, heavy cream, and stevia in a blender. Add the sliced strawberries, cover, and blend on high or until smooth with bits of strawberries still intact.

Pour the mixture into four ice pop molds and attach the sticks. Freeze for at least 1 hour, preferably overnight. Serve frozen.

Nutritional Information per Serving

Calories: 120

Fat: 19 g

Protein: 8 g

Carbohydrates: 1 g

Fiber: 1.4 g

Butter Dark Chocolate Brownies

Chocolate lovers, rejoice! This decadent dessert is the perfect cure for that chocolate urge when you are on the Keto diet. By replacing high carb wheat flour with almond flour, you do not have to feel guilty for indulging in a brownie or two. On an extra special occasion, add a large dollop of Creamy Choco Coconut Cream. You deserve it.

Number of Servings: 4 (2 brownies per serving)

You will Need:

- 3 large organic eggs
- ¾ cup almond flour
- ¼ cup chopped dark chocolate (90% cacao)
- ½ cup stevia
- 4 Tbsp. melted and cooled grass-fed butter
- 3 Tbsp. unsweetened cocoa powder
- 1 tsp. pure vanilla extract
- ½ tsp. baking powder
- ¼ tsp. sea salt

How to Prepare:

Set the oven to 350 degrees F to preheat. Line a baking pan with parchment paper and set aside.

In a mixing bowl, mix together the almond flour, cocoa powder, baking powder, stevia, and salt. Mix well.

In a separate bowl, beat the eggs until foamy. Add the melted butter and pure vanilla extract then stir until evenly combined.

Create a small pit in the center of the flour mixture and pour in the egg mixture. Fold everything until evenly combined.

Add the chopped chocolate into the mixture until the chocolate is evenly distributed. Spread the batter in the prepared baking pan.

Bake the batter for 30 minutes or until done. Insert a toothpick in the center of the brownie. If it comes out clean, it is ready.

Carefully remove the brownie from the oven and place on a cooling rack. Allow to set for about 5 minutes then slice into 8 pieces. Serve warm, or store in an airtight container and refrigerate for up to a week.

Nutritional Information per Serving

Calories: 382

Fat: 34.4 g

Protein: 6.4 g

Carbohydrates: 5.8 g

Fiber: 5.2 g

BUTTER PECAN BITES

Pecans are rich in healthy fats, dietary fiber, potassium, magnesium, and iron. Smothered in butter and baked to perfection, these delectable dessert bars can also be served as energy snacks on busy days.

Number of Servings: 4 (4 pieces per serving)

You will Need:

- 2 large organic eggs
- 1 cup chopped pecans
- ½ cup grass-fed butter
- ¼ cup almond meal
- ¼ cup almond flour
- ¼ cup blackstrap molasses
- ½ tsp. pure vanilla extract
- Coconut cooking oil spray, as needed

How to Prepare:

Set the oven to 325 degrees F to preheat. Lightly coat a square baking pan with coconut oil cooking spray and set aside.

Place the butter into a microwaveable bowl and microwave for 50 seconds or until melted. Add the blackstrap molasses and stir well. Set aside to cool.

Meanwhile, beat the eggs and pure vanilla extract in a mixing bowl. Once the butter mixture is cooled, whisk it into the egg mixture until smooth.

Gradually mix the almond meal and flour into the egg mixture until a soft dough forms. Fold in the pecans and mix until evenly distributed.

Spread the batter in the prepared baking pan. Tap the batter against the kitchen counter to eliminate air pockets.

Bake the batter for 15 to 20 minutes, or until the butter pecan batter becomes golden brown and firm. Insert a toothpick in the center of the batter; if it comes out clean, it is ready.

Place on a cooling rack and allow to cool for 10 minutes. After that, slice into 16 pieces and store in an airtight container. Best served warm with a dollop of cream cheese or whipped cream.

Nutritional Information per Serving

Calories: 636

Fat: 36 g

Protein: 12 g

Carbohydrates: 28 g

Fiber: 3 g

CRISPY CHOCOLATE-COATED BACON

The Keto diet is a major challenge to those with an insatiable sweet tooth. If you happen to be one of those, then you will find this sinful little dessert more than comforting. Just take care not to overindulge yourself, otherwise you will end up gaining more weight than losing it in the diet. The key here is to just nibble a little bit after a healthy meal.

Number of Servings: 4

You will Need:

- **16 organic, grass-fed bacon strips**
- **6 Tbsp. chopped unsweetened chocolate (85% cacao)**
- **3 Tbsp. coconut oil**
- **2 tsp. stevia**

How to Prepare:

Set the oven to 425 degrees F to preheat.

Lay the bacon strips on a baking sheet and bake for 15 minutes, or until crisp and browned all over. Transfer to a cooling rack and allow to cool completely.

In the meantime, place a saucepan over low flame and add the coconut oil and chopped unsweetened chocolate. Stir until melted then add the stevia and mix well. Turn off the heat.

Place the bacon strips on a sheet of parchment paper and spoon the coconut oil and chocolate mixture on top. Turn over the bacon strips and coat again.

Transfer to a platter and refrigerate for about an hour. Best serve chilled.

Nutritional Information per Serving

Calories: 428

Fat: 25.6 g

Protein: 18.8 g

Carbohydrates: 3.6 g

Fiber: 2.8 g

MINI RASPBERRY CREAM CHEESE BALLS

Who needs candy when you have got cold little cream cheese balls with more than a tinge of fresh raspberry waiting for you at home? Enjoy this sweet treat as an afternoon snack or a refreshing dessert after dinner.

Number of Servings: 4 (2 cream cheese balls per serving)

You will Need:

- 2 ½ Tbsp. fresh or frozen organic raspberries
- 2 ½ Tbsp. cream cheese
- 2 Tbsp. grass-fed butter
- 2 Tbsp. coconut oil
- 2 Tbsp. heavy cream
- ½ tsp. pure vanilla extract

How to Prepare:

Pour the raspberries into a blender and add the vanilla extract. Blend until finely chopped. Set aside.

Combine the coconut oil, butter, and cream cheese in a microwaveable bowl. Cover and microwave for 10 seconds on high. Stir and microwave again up to 3 times, or until melted.

Carefully remove the bowl from the microwave and stir in the heavy cream. Add the blended raspberry and vanilla extract mixture, mixing well.

Cover the bowl and refrigerate for 30 minutes, or until chilled and slightly firm. Divide into 8 small balls. Arrange the balls on a platter and freeze for at least 1 hour. Best served chilled.

Nutritional Information per Serving

Calories: 162

Fat: 18 g

Protein: 0.8 g

Carbohydrates: 0.8 g

Fiber: 0.8 g

KETO COFFEE CHOCOLATE CHIP COOKIES

Everyone loves chocolate chip cookies, and this Keto version is just as scrumptious as the classic one. The espresso twist also gives it a charmingly robust flavor. Enjoy these cookies with hot milk as a late night snack or dessert, or – if you are looking for a major coffee fix – in the morning with some buttered coffee.

Number of Servings: 4 (4 large cookies per serving)

You will Need:

- 2 large organic eggs
- 6 oz. unsweetened chocolate chips
- ½ cup unsweetened cocoa powder
- ½ cup vanilla whey protein powder
- ½ cup grass-fed butter
- ¼ cup almond meal
- ¼ cup water
- 1 Tbsp. regular or decaf coffee crystals
- 1 tsp. stevia
- ½ tsp. sea salt
- Coconut oil cooking spray, as needed

How to Prepare:

Set the oven to 350 degrees F to preheat. Lightly coat the baking sheet with the coconut oil cooking spray and set aside.

Combine the stevia, vanilla whey protein powder, almond meal, cocoa powder, instant coffee crystals, and sea salt in a food processor. Process until combined.

Transfer the mixture into a bowl and cut the butter into the mixture. Mix in the eggs, one at a time, followed by the water. Mix well. Fold in the chocolate chips.

Divide the batter into 16 cookie dough balls and then arrange them on the baking sheet. Make sure to leave at least 2 inches of space between each.

Bake for 15 minutes, or until the cookies are slightly firm and golden brown.

Place on a cooling rack and let stand for 5 minutes. Store in an airtight container. Serve warm or cool.

Nutritional Information per Serving

Calories:

Fat: 37 g

Protein: 16 g

Carbohydrates: 12 g

Fiber: 4 g

COCONUT LIME BUTTER BALLS

Here is a quick and easy Keto dessert recipe you can make at home to get rid of your hunger pangs. The great thing about this recipe is you can also replace lime with vanilla extract, almond extract, cinnamon, lemon, or even berries. Your creativity is your limit!

Number of Servings: 4 (2 butter balls per serving)

You will Need:

- 2 Tbsp. coconut oil
- 2 Tbsp. grass-fed butter
- 2 Tbsp. heavy cream
- 1 ½ Tbsp. unsweetened shredded coconut flakes
- 1 Tbsp. freshly squeezed lime juice
- ½ tsp. stevia
- 1 oz. cream cheese

How to Prepare:

Combine the coconut oil, butter, and cream cheese in a microwaveable bowl. Cover and microwave for 10 seconds on high. Stir and microwave again up to 3 times, or until melted.

Carefully remove the bowl from the microwave and stir in the heavy cream. Add the freshly squeezed lime juice and stevia, mixing well.

Cover the bowl and refrigerate for 30 minutes, or until chilled and slightly firm. Divide into 8 small balls.

Spread the shredded coconut flakes on a plate and coat the butter balls with them. Arrange the balls on a platter and freeze for at least 1 hour. Best served chilled.

Nutritional Information per Serving

Calories: 162

Fat: 18 g

Protein: 0.8 g

Carbohydrates: 0.8 g

Fiber: 0.8 g

KETO GINGERSNAPS

This low carb version of the classic ginger and cinnamon cookies is packed with healthy fats from the butter, coconut oil, and almond meal, and protein from whey protein and egg. Serve these gingersnaps fresh with hot milk or buttered coffee for an extra cozy vibe.

Number of Servings: 4 (5 cookies per serving)

You will Need:

- 1 organic egg
- ½ cup almond meal
- ½ cup vanilla whey protein powder
- ¼ cup blackstrap molasses
- ¼ cup coconut oil
- 2 Tbsp. grass-fed butter
- 2 tsp. gluten
- 1 tsp. baking soda
- 1 tsp. cinnamon
- ½ tsp. ground ginger
- ¼ tsp. ground cinnamon
- ¼ tsp. sea salt

How to Prepare:

Set the oven at 350 degrees F to preheat.

Combine the butter, coconut oil, blackstrap molasses, and egg in an electric mixer. Blend well until fluffy and creamy.

Gradually mix in the almond meal, gluten, and vanilla whey protein powder. Add the baking soda, salt, ginger, cinnamon, and cloves.

Mix well into a soft dough.

Using a tablespoon, scoop the dough into small balls on a dry baking sheet. Leave about 2 inches of spaces between each cookie dough ball.

Bake for 8 minutes, or until the gingersnaps are golden brown. Set on a cooling rack for 5 minutes then serve. Store leftovers in an airtight container.

Nutritional Information per Serving

Calories: 380

Fat: 15 g

Protein: 21 g

Carbohydrates: 6 g

Fiber: 1 g

PEANUT BUTTER AND CREAM CHEESE CHEWIES

These scrumptious peanut butter and cream cheese treats have a crispy outer shell with chewy and gooey insides. Enjoy one after a savory meal for something a little sweet. These are also fun to make, so you might want to make them with your family or friends as a little get together.

Number of Servings: 4 (5 cookies per serving)

You will Need:

- 1 large organic egg
- ¾ cup organic, sugar-free peanut butter
- ½ cup cream cheese, at room temperature
- 15 drops liquid stevia
- ¾ tsp. pure vanilla extract

How to Prepare:

Set the oven to 350 degrees F to preheat. Line a baking sheet with parchment paper and set aside.

In a bowl, mix together the peanut butter, cream cheese, egg, liquid stevia, and pure vanilla extract. Stir until completely combined.

Cover the bowl with a plastic wrap and chill for 15 minutes. This will make it easier for you to form the dough into cookies.

After chilling, remove the dough from the refrigerator and divide into 20 1-inch sized pieces. Arrange the pieces on the prepared baking sheet, leaving 1 ½ inches of space in between each.

Flatten the dough balls slightly with the back of a spoon or fork. Then, bake for 12 minutes, or until golden brown.

Place the baking sheet of Peanut Butter and Cream Cheese Chewies on a cooling rack. Let stand for 5 minutes then transfer into an airtight container.

Nutritional Information per Serving

Calories: 395

Fat: 6.9 g

Protein: 3.1 g

Carbohydrates: 1.6 g

Fiber: 0.6 g

CONCLUSION:

Now that you have obtained a large collection of Keto-friendly recipes as well as four 7-day meal plans, the only thing left for you to do is to get started!

So, go ahead and schedule an appointment with your doctor or licensed dietician right now. Find out more about the Keto diet and determine whether you can start it and how. Next, get rid of all the sugar and grains from your kitchen and replace them with Keto-approved ingredients.

After that, you can finally create your meal plans, gather your ingredients, and start cooking! The sooner you take steps towards weight loss, the sooner you will achieve your health goals.

OTHER BOOKS BY VIRGINIA HOFFMAN

DID YOU ENJOY THIS BOOK?

I want to thank you for purchasing and reading this book. I really hope you got a lot out of it.

Can I ask a quick favor though?

If you enjoyed this book I would really appreciate it if you could leave me a positive review on Amazon.

I love getting feedback from my customers and reviews on Amazon really do make a difference. I read all my reviews and would really appreciate your thoughts.

Thanks so much.

VIRGINIA HOFFMAN

CPSIA information can be obtained
at www.ICGtesting.com
Printed in the USA
FSHW021307270420
69654FS

9 781521 359167